The Far Western Frontier

The Far Western Frontier

Advisory Editor

RAY A. BILLINGTON

Senior Research Associate
at the Henry E. Huntington Library
and Art Gallery

TEXAS.

OBSERVATIONS,

HISTORICAL, GEOGRAPHICAL AND DESCRIPTIVE

BY MRS. MARY AUSTIN HOLLEY

ARNO PRESS
A NEW YORK TIMES COMPANY
New York • 1973

Reprint Edition 1973 by Arno Press Inc.

Reprinted from a copy in The State
Historical Society of Wisconsin Library

The Far Western Frontier
ISBN for complete set: 0-405-04955-2
See last pages of this volume for titles.

Manufactured in the United States of America

Library of Congress Cataloging in Publication Data

Holley, Mary Austin, 1784-1846.
   Texas; observations, historical, geographical and
descriptive, in a series of letters.

   (The Far Western frontier)
   Reprint of the 1833 ed.
   1. Texas--Description and travel. 2. Texas--
History--To 1846--Sources. I. Series.
F389.H73 1973   917.64'03'3   72-9451
ISBN 0-405-04979-X

TEXAS.

OBSERVATIONS,

HISTORICAL, GEOGRAPHICAL AND DESCRIPTIVE,

In a Series of Letters,

Written during a Visit to Austin's Colony, with a view to a permanent
settlement in that country, in the Autumn of 1831.

BY MRS. MARY AUSTIN HOLLEY.

WITH AN APPENDIX,

Containing specific answers to certain questions, relative to Coloniza
tion in Texas, issued some time since by the London Geographical
Society. Also, some notice of the recent political events in that
quarter.

BALTIMORE:
ARMSTRONG & PLASKITT.
1833.

PRINTED BY J. W. WOODS,

I, N. Calvert street.

TO

Col. STEPHEN F. AUSTIN.

Dear Sir,

Too much praise cannot be awarded
to you, for your judicious, disinterested and generous management, of the affairs of your Colony.
You have accomplished great ends with small
means. You have endured more hardships, and
made greater sacrifices, than often falls to the lot
of man to encounter. You have a right, not only
to that best reward, the consciousness of good
deeds done—but to a just appreciation of those
deeds by the public.

There is great pleasure, therefore, in inscrib-
ing to you, as a humble tribute to distinguished
merit, this little work on your own Texas, by
your friend and kinswoman.

MARY AUSTIN HOLLEY.

Bolivar, Texas, December 24, 1831.

INTRODUCTION.

Texas, until within the last few years, has been, literally, a terra incognita. That such a region existed, has, indeed, been known; but in respect to its geography and natural resources, clouds and darkness have rested upon it. This is the more remarkable, lying as it does, contiguous to two enlightened nations, the United States, on the one side, and Mexico, on the other; being, moreover, very easy of access, both by land and sea. While Britons, impelled by a daring spirit of enterprise, have penetrated to the ice-bound region of Melville's Island, and our own New Englanders have encountered all the hardships and hazards of the western desert, the Rocky Mountains and hostile Indians, to find a home at the mouth of Columbia river, this most inviting region, lying just at their doors, has been altogether overlooked. Quite unexpectedly, as it were, a report has reached the public ear, that

1*

the country lying west of the Sabine river, is a
tract of surpassing beauty, exceeding even our
best western lands in productiveness, with a
climate perfectly salubrious, and of a tempera-
ture, at all seasons of the year, most delightful.
The admirers of this new country, speaking from
actual knowledge, and a personal inspection, are
not content, in their descriptions of it, to make
use of ordinary terms of commendation.   They
hesitate not to call it a *splendid* country—an enchanting spot.   It would seem as if enchantment
had, indeed, thrown its spell over their minds,
for, with very few exceptions, all who return
from this fairy land, are perfect enthusiasts in
their admiration of it.   Whatever qualifications
to its excellence, the most cautious of them are
disposed to make, have reference to those inconveniences, which unavoidably pertain to every
country in the incipient stages of its settlement.

So apparently extravagant have been the representations of the natural beauty and resources
of this country, that many persons are incredu-
lous, and attribute them to the schemes of interested contractors, eager to allure the unwary
emigrant, by deceptive statements.   Such a motive, if it really actuates the conduct of any one,

cannot be, too severely, condemned. A design more criminal and disgraceful cannot be, easily, conceived of, and ought not to be lightly insinuated against respectable men. What design more cruel, than that of deliberately seducing, not the confiding emigrant alone, but, with him, his wife and children, to become the certain victims of privation, disappointment and ultimate ruin, in the wilderness. The character and respectability of the witnesses above referred to, at once, repel an insinuation so atrocious.

While listening, for the first time, to the favourable reports of Texas, it must be confessed, a suspicion is very apt to arise in the mind, that so much imputed excellence if it really existed, could not have been so long concealed from the view of the world; and we are prone to ask, how has it happened, that a territory, possessing such uncommon advantage of climate and soil, has not been explored and appropriated before. To this very natural inquiry, a satisfactory answer is at hand.

Two causes seem to have operated to prevent the earlier settlement of the province of Texas, and to retard the developement of its resources. In the first place, the jealous policy of the old

Spanish government, uniformly discouraged all attempts to penetrate into the country. It was the policy of the government, that completely locked up Texas, and all the Spanish American possessions, and excluded even visiters and travellers. It was a favourite saying of the Spanish Captain General of the internal provinces, Don Nemisio Salcedo, that he would stop the birds from flying over the boundary line between Texas and the United States, if it were in his power. This rigid policy prevented any one from attempting to explore the country by land, for perpetual imprisonment was the inevitable result of detection and capture.

In the second place, the Carancahua Indians, who inhabited the coast, were represented to be of a character, uncommonly ferocious. They were, popularly, believed to be cannibals, and many tales of most frightful import, were told, of them; such as, if true, it must be acknowledged, were sufficiently appaling to check the enterprise, and damp the ardour of the most eager adventurer. These representations of the character of the Carancahuas, though, in a measure true, were, greatly, exaggerated; and it is believed by many, that they were either fabricated

or at least countenanced, by the Spanish authorities, to prevent intercourse with the Province,
which it was not easy to guard by a military
force. Thus, the whole of this country remained for ages unknown to the world, and instead
of being converted into an abode of industrious
and happy freemen, as it might have been, it was
doomed by the selfishness of men, to continue a
howling wilderness. No maps, charts or geographical notices, were ever allowed by the
Spaniards to be taken of it. The map, compiled
by Col. Austin, and published by Tanner, is the
first and only correct geographical information of
the country, that has been ever published. The
persons who were engaged in the expeditions
under Generals Bernardo, Guitierrez and Toledo,
in 1812–13, knew nothing of Texas, except
along and near, the road they travelled, for they
were too much occupied, by the war, during the
short time, they had possession, to explore the
country. It is uncertain how long this extensive
and valuable country would have remained unknown and unsettled, had not the bold enterprise
and perseverance of the Austins, torn away the
veil that hid it from the view of the world, and
redeemed it from the wilderness, by the settle-

ment of a flourishing colony of North Americans, on the Brazos and Colorado rivers.   With the settlement of this colony, a new era has dawned upon Texas.   The natural riches of this beautiful Province have begun to be unfolded, and its charms displayed, to the eyes of admiring adventurers.   A new island, as it were, has been discovered, in these latter days, at our very doors, apparently fresh from the hands of its Maker, and adapted, beyond most lands, both to delight the senses, and enrich the pockets, of those, who are disposed to accept of its bounties.

Without any assistance from the government, or fostering care of any sort, but simply under a permission to enter, some thousands of industrious farmers and mechanics, with their families, have already located themselves here.   Their numbers are rapidly increasing, and there cannot be a doubt, that, in a few years, Texas will become one of the most thriving, if not the most populous, of the Mexican States.

Of the numerous contracts for purposes of colonization, made by the Mexican Government with individuals and companies, few of those of early date, for causes, which it is not necessary now to mention, have proved successful, while that of Col. Austin, to which the following letters have especial reference, has been eminently so. The author of these letters, made a visit of observation to this colony, in the autumn of 1831, with a view to the ultimate settlement of herself and family. Many of her friends did not hesitate to condemn the enterprise as romantic, and too adventurous for a female. Allured however, by the flattering representations of the country, made to her, by persons in whose judgment she placed implicit confidence, and tempted by the very liberal terms of settlement proposed by the colonization laws; but, above all, impelled by a desire, which every widowed mother will know how to appreciate, of making some provision for an only son, a provision, which, if not immediately available, cannot fail to be ample, at some future day; favoured, also, by a previous personal acquaintance with Col. Austin himself, and encouraged by a brother already established in the country, she resolved to go. But previous to a final removal from her native land, prudence dictated, that she should first cast an eye of observation over the ground, the probable scene of her future weal or woe.

The result of her expedition was, a decided
purpose of removal, as soon as domestic arrangements would permit. Her most sanguine im-
pressions of the natural advantages of the country,
both with regard to the salubrity of the climate,
the fertility of the soil, and the facility with which
the lands can be brought under cultivation, were
confirmed, and, without further hesitation, she
determined to choose this spot for her home.

To the enterprising public, especially to emigrants, the following letters, in the hope of being
useful, are respectfully presented.

The publication of them was suggested, by
the notice of some queries, by the London Geographical Society, regarding the localities, the
moral and physical capabilities and prospects of
Texas, with a view to emigration, to which queries a distinct, and it is believed, satisfactory reply, will be found, in the subsequent pages.   The
commands of numerous friends, to whom a visit
to Texas seemed little less marvellous, than the
wanderings of Dante on the other side of the Styx,
enjoined upon her, *to observe and tell them all about
the country*, and to assure them, whether it were,
or were not, a *fabulous land*.

The public mind, seemed to require, more just, more distinct, and detailed information, than had, hitherto, been given: many persons, disposed to emigrate to this fair portion of the earth, needed assurance, that the natives do not *kill and eat people* there, nor always insult and rob them. It has been thought, that an exact representation of things, *just as they are,* in this beautiful and fertile country, where the greatest abundance of all valuable and substantial possessions, are the easy and certain reward of industry and perseverance, would be acceptable.

Emigration is, often, undertaken with expectations so vague and preposterous, that, disappointment, if not ruin, is the inevitable consequence. Not more unreasonable were the emigrants of the early history of America, who expected to find streets, paved with gold, because that metal abounds in the mines of Mexico and Peru, than are those individuals of the present day, who, escaping from confinement and poverty in the northern cities of America, or from the slavery and wretchedness of the crowded and oppressed communities of Europe, complain of their disappointments in Texas, because, forsooth, they do not find in Brazoria and San Felipe, the Phi-

2

ladelphia market and streets lighted with gas.
Such persons would do well to ask themselves, in
what part of the world, they can get land for
nothing?—where obtain so many enjoyments, with
so little labour? What region combines every
good?

The idle and the vicious, as it happens every
where, will be sure to be disappointed in Texas.
Like the hero of Milton, such characters carry
their discontent with them.

A soil, that yields the fruits of nearly every
latitude, almost spontaneously, with a climate of
perpetual summer, must, like that of other countries, have a seed-time and a harvest. Though
the land be, literally flowing with milk and honey, yet, the cows must be milked, and the honey
must be gathered. Houses must be built and
enclosures made. The deer must be hunted, and
the fish must be caught. From the primeval
curse, that, in the sweat of his brow, man shall
eat bread, though its severity be mollified, there
is no exemption, even here. The emigrant should
bear in mind, that in a new community, *labour* is
the most valuable commodity. He sees about
him, all the means for supplying, not only the
necessaries, but also, the comforts and luxuries of

life. It is his part, to apply them to his use. He is, abundantly, furnished, with the raw materials; but his hands must mould them into the forms of art.

With a view to emigrant mothers, on whom the comfort of every family, and the general well-being of the infant colony, so much depends, it has been thought that, a journal in detail, of one of themselves, would furnish more hints for the judicious arrangements of the voyage and the indispensable attentions to the comfort and economy of an infant establishment, than could be gathered from the more abstract and general views of gentleman travellers. Many trivial circumstances are, therefore, introduced, not with a view to *amuse*, but to be applied to some useful end. Much incident, calculated to interest the general reader, is not to be expected. But the author having ample means of information, may, without vanity, indulge one hope, as she professes but one aim—utility.

LETTER I.

Bolivar, Texas, December, 1831.

I hasten, my dear C——, to comply with my promise of giving you a full and detailed account of my movements during my visit to Texas. I shall first give you an account of my voyage; you shall then be informed of all I have seen with my own eyes, and of all I have learned from others, respecting this interesting country. I will not promise to be too concise, and you may, perhaps, find, that you have got more than you bargained for. I have seen and heard much that interests me exceedingly, and it is likely, I shall have much to say; I hope you will be patient and hear my story out. Of this you may rest assured, that I will write nothing which I did not either see with my own eyes, or learn from sources which commanded my entire confidence. You may perhaps surmise, that my journey into the province was too short to admit of much incident or observation. As for that matter, I might have travelled farther and learned less. What useful knowledge was to

2*

be gathered by traversing the unbroken wilderness, or gazing upon the boundless prairie? I might have seen more trees, more Indians, and more wild beasts. I consider myself most fortunate, indeed, in having met, so soon after my arrival in the colony, with the very persons, who, doubtless, are more competent, than any other individuals living, to give the information I desired; men who had, personally, inspected the land, in its length and breadth, had explored its rivers, and surveyed its coast; men who were perfectly familiar with its whole history from the beginning, and were the best judges that could be, of its present capabilities, and future prospects. I need not say, that one of these gentlemen, was Col. Austin himself. But, I will not anticipate, so, to begin with my voyage.

I took passage, for the Colony, in the schooner Spica, sixty tons, captain D——. A larger vessel would not answer for the navigation of the Brazos, on account of a troublesome bar, at the mouth of the river. I was, therefore, obliged to content myself, with small accommodations. They were, however, neat and comfortable. The cabin, appropriated to the ladies, had but two berths, which had been taken by two of my

fellow travellers, one of which had several children.   A lodging place, was, therefore, arranged
for me, on the transom, far more comfortable,
and with a better circulation of air, than the
berths afforded.   Another lady joined us, afterwards, and our little cabin, as you may well suppose, was completely filled, with ourselves and
baggage.

The captain was a Bostonian, polite and
agreeable, and what was yet more to the purpose in hand, an excellent seaman.   He had
been in the India and Mediterranean trade, and in
the service of the United States as commander
of a Revenue Cutter.   He had been recently
reformed out of office, as the phrase is.   But
having known many honest citizens in the same
predicament, we were not the more distrustful
of him on that account.   It was a satisfaction to
know that he had seen service, and was a seaman
of experience, for our voyage, though short, is,
sometimes, not without hazard, on account of the
*Northers;** as they are called.   The passengers,
though   strangers,   were   respectable,   and   I
promised myself a safe and agreeable trip.

_____

*A troublesome wind on the coast, about which I will tell you
something by and by.

I was on board at the time appointed, Tuesday, October 18, at three o'clock. We were to sail at four. All hands were punctual—every thing ready. I took my seat, with the other passengers on deck, engaged in conversation with some friends, while waiting for the tow steamer, to conduct us to the mouth of the Mississippi. Thus occupied, I did not regard the lapse of time, until the sun went down, and no steamer came. My attention was aroused, by a philippic of our captain, against a certain class of people in New Orleans, for their faithlessness, and utter disregard of their engagements. He was, however, extremely moderate, considering the disappointment, inconvenience and delay, we were about to suffer. It was now too late to proceed for this day. The musquetos were troublesome. There was no alternative, but to go on shore: which most of us did, with the utmost good nature, not much displeased, in fact, with the prospect of one more night, of comfortable repose, without *rocking*. So here is good night to you. We will take a fresh start in the morning.

Affectionately, yours.

LETTER II.

Bolivar, Texas, Dec. 1831.

THE next day, at the appointed hour, we were all at our quarters. The captain of the tow-boat sent word, that he would be along for us about sun-set. But, our captain doubtless thinking one good turn deserves another, without giving him notice, made a different arrangement, and before that time, we were attached to the smoking sides of the *Shark*, balanced by another schooner on the opposite side, and under way for sea.

The skies were soft—our spirits buoyant, and under the influence of sanguine hopes, we were willing to consider these little delays, as the most serious, if not the most amusing, of our adventures. We moved smoothly down the current, during a glowing sun-set, succeeded by a full moon, giving a romantic beauty to the luxuriant and cultivated shores.

I had now, an opportunity to notice my fellow travellers. They were all bound, like myself, to *the land of promise,* on a tour of observation, with

reference to a permanent residence.　A better as-
sortment of professions and character, for an infant colony, could not have been selected.　An
editor of a gazette from Michigan—a civil en-
gineer, from Kentucky—a trader from Missouri,
with his bride along, and an outfit of dry goods—
a genteel good looking widow, on a visit to her
son—with a suitable proportion of the working
class.

At day-light, the next morning, the tow-boat
left us, to pursue our solitary course, in the great
gulph, which spread its deep waters before us.
We pressed onward, while she tacked about, to
offer assistance to a ship and four brigs, which
were waiting for an escort to the city we had
left.

We stood out for sea, with a gentle breeze
from the south-east.　Soon we were sensible of
the change of motion.　We began to find it difficult to preserve our equilibrium, and very shortly, most of us were compelled to yield to the
sickening influence of the sea, our sufferings from
this cause, being not a little aggravated by the
pitchings and tossings, of so small a vessel.　My
mattress was spread on deck, for I could not en-
dure the closeness of the cabin.　Under other

circumstances, what a delightful situation was this for contemplation. The resplendent sky above, around me, on every side, the sea, ever glorious and beautiful. But, nothing, just then, was capable of inspiring me with sentimental emotions, nothing could counteract the morbid sensations which oppressed both my body and mind. The other ladies and some of the gentlemen, were in the same predicament, making a most poetical group—poetry, after the Hogarth school.

Our progress was rapid. We met no sail, and encountered no adventure. On the evening of the second day we had a gale, sufficiently violent to frighten ladies, but not so much so as to endanger the vessel, the wind blowing off shore. The storm was soon over, leaving a swelling sea. I cannot say that night was the most agreeable I ever passed, being prostrated by sickness, and having eaten nothing for two days. I would advise all who take this voyage, to carry a liberal supply of oranges with them. This fruit is most refreshing to the lips, and has a relish, when every other article of food seems insipid.

The morning of October 22d, was fair and bright, and land to our great joy was announced.

After dinner, the mouth of the Brazos lay before
us.   It was less than three days, since we parted
from the levee, in New Orleans.   We cast anchor and sent off a boat for a pilot, and to take
soundings on the bar.   The pilot came on board.
He is an American, of gentlemanly deportment,
and lives at the point of land, formed by the
Brazos with the gulf.   Here there is a Mexican
garrison, and the tri-colored flag is hoisted, the
first signal of our approach to a foreign land.
He reported, that in consequence of the high
wind, the night before, there were but four feet
of water on the bar, that tide, and the Spica,
drawing six feet, it would be necessary for us to
remain where we were, until the next morning,
when he would conduct us over.

We had now leisure to survey our position—
to recover our spirits and the use of our feet; to
fish and amuse ourselves, and to enjoy the grateful
feelings which succeed to moments of suffering
and danger.

On our right, in front of their palmetto-roof-
ed, and windowless barracks, the lazy sentinels
were "walking their lonely rounds," without ex-
cessive martial parade; nor did the unturretted
quarters of the commanding officer, show forth

much of the blazonry of a Spanish Don. There was no tree, no cultivation. A uniform verdure, alone, indicated the season of the year. Nothing marked civilization, save a fabric for making salt; itself an image of desolation, and the solitary house of the pilot, standing high on piles, serving, at once, for a beacon for the mariner, and a refuge from the storm. The whole appearance of the scene, at the north, with the associations of a northern climate, would be called bleak; but in this latitude, the dark blue sea, when not made terrific by a storm, always suggests agreeable images to the mind, especially that of a refreshing coolness.

We amused ourselves, while lying here, with dissecting some of those curious links, between the vegetable and animal kingdoms, called sun-fish. They were large and delicately white and transparent; formed, not unlike a flower of the rose shape, partially expanded, and placed in a saucer. At first view, one is disposed to call it a vegetable; but, on applying the knife, it shrinks and quivers, as from a sensation of pain, especially, the saucer part of it. The saucer, is obviously and beautifully designed by its author, as a boat for the little mariner. The collapsing,

3

however, is not so violent as that of the sensitive plant, when touched. We spent the evening, not unpleasantly, singing our first vespers in this Catholic land.

Affectionately, yours, &c.

LETTER III.

Bolivar, Texas, December, 1831.

THE moment the tide would answer, next day, it was not, however, till after dinner, the pilot was on board. In a few minutes, we were safely over the bar, for it is not wide, but not without some severe rubs and pitches. The tide, always irregular, had not yet recovered from the influence of the storm, nor attained its usual height, though there was no hope of its being higher, that day. This bar presents a serious obstruction to the navigation of the river. Vessels have been, indeed, wrecked, in crossing it, and none but strong vessels, or such as are of light draught, should attempt it. It is to be hoped, and may be, reasonably expected, that, when an extended commerce will justify the expense, this bar will be, in a good measure, removed by the hand of art.

This bar is not peculiar to the Brazos river. Bars are common to all the rivers of this coast. They are formed by the prevalence of the southerly winds, which act in a direction contrary to that of the stream, and by checking and dispersing the current, cause a deposite of the sand, which the water brings with it.

Vessels arriving after the commencement of the northers, as they are called, which is, generally, about the last of November, are sometimes blown off to sea, for weeks. When they return to the coast, there is much danger, that the southern breezes, not always gently blowing, may dash them against the bar. The moment of arrival, therefore, is a moment of great anxiety, as well as of joy, and all hands pray for fair weather, and *whistle for favouring gales.** We were, therefore, sufficiently happy, as we doubtless had much reason to be piously thankful, when we found ourselves safe, upon the bosom of this beautiful river.

El Brazos de Dios, in Spanish, means: "The

* "Whistle to St. Antonio for a fair wind," is a familiar expression of the sailors and boatmen. "The Brazos boat song," adopts this expression.

arms of God." It is on many accounts, a most
interesting river, and has one peculiarity which is
very remarkable.   Its head waters spring in the
Comanche country, and consequently, are but
little known.   It has the very peculiar feature, in
one of its branches, which has no parallel in any
part of the world—a salt water river running
from the interior towards the sea.

The westernmost branch has its source, in an
extensive salt region, not Mr. Jefferson's *Salt
Mountain*, of which so much was said and sung,
at the time of the Louisiana purchase, but a vast
plain, of one or two hundred miles, in extent, the
land of which, is charged with mineral salt, and
on which nitre is deposited by the atmosphere.
The rains dissolve this salt.   When, in the dry
season, the water is evaporated, the salt is deposited, in immense quantities, and the whole
plain is covered with chrystalized salt.   When,
on the other hand the rains are copious, an extensive, shallow, temporary lake is formed, which
discharges its briny water into the Brazos, by
the *Salt Branch*, as it is called, its waters, being
at times salt enough to pickle pork.

The freshet produced in the Brazos, by the
rise of the Salt Branch, renders the whole river,
for a while, brackish, and its waters bring with

them a fine red clay, as slippery as soap, and as
sticky as putty. This clay is deposited, on the
shores of the river, and retains its saltness, as
does the water its brackish, or slightly saltish,
taste, until a freshet produced by the fresh
branches, washes it away, or covers it up, when
the river becomes fresh and potable, and continues so, until another rise in the salt branch.

We came to, before the door of the pilot's
house, which fronts the stream. The officer of
the garrison boarded us, to examine our passports;
a ceremony, the Mexicans are very tenacious of,
from their known jealousy of foreigners. He
was a young man, dark and rather handsome, in
a neat Mexican uniform, probably his dress-suit;
for occasions of so much company, are not of
every day occurrence, on this station. He very
politely, addressed our captain, in a few words
of English, probably, his whole vocabulary;
while the latter displayed to best advantage, in
reply, his whole stock of Spanish. Saluting us
gracefully, as he passed, the business of passports
was soon adjusted in the cabin. Ours were spoken
of, and inquired about; but with courtly com-
plaisance, and gallant reliance upon a lady's word,
he waived the ceremony of examination, and
3*

saved us the trouble of searching our trunks for
them.

Our sails were now spread to a fair, light
breeze, upon the Brazos. We proceeded gaily,
with the accession of spirits, our good fortune
had inspired, for about four miles. The river,
for that distance is deep, but partially obstructed,
at one spot, by a sunken vessel. The average
width of the Brazos, from its mouth, to Bolivar,
is about fifty yards. Its average depth, from
three to five fathoms. A slight flaw of wind
took us, suddenly, too far towards the left bank;
the tide left us, and there we stuck fast. Here
we remained another day, waiting for the evening
tide. Though impatient to proceed, we made a
virtue of necessity, and did not permit the hours
to drag heavily upon our hands. The gentlemen
went ashore to hunt, and the ladies amused themselves with fishing. Wild fowl of every description, were continually passing over our
heads, while ducks, snipe and curlews, were in
constant motion, among the high grass of the
shore.

The next tide, happily, took us from our
moorings and our sports, and soon opened to us,

the most beautiful river scenery, I ever beheld:
and I have travelled,

" From Mexico to lake Champlain,"
" From Maine to Mississippi shore."

The alternate woodland and prairie, which
make the peculiar beauty of a Texas landscape,
commenced, with small intervals: now the glossy
boughs of the one, hanging over the river's brink,
and now the rich grass of the other, extending,
as far as the eye could reach.   Nothing was
wanting, but neat white dwellings, to complete
the picture.   The lawns were as smooth as art
could make them, and the trees, sometimes in
clumps, sometimes in avenues, seemed to display
the hand of taste.   The sun and the air, seemed
brighter and softer, than elsewhere.   We were,
all enchanted with Texas, and, with one accord
exclaimed,

"This is the spot, and here I wish to live,"
"Despising all that wealth and power can give."

Thus we moved onward, through a day of
gentle pleasure, feeling, as if we, alone, were the
possessors, of this beautiful creation: for we saw
not a human creature, nor any trace of one.   We
admired the variety of foliage, much of which

was new to us, all in the hues of spring, and the graceful windings of the river. There is nothing in the whole course of the Ohio and Mississippi, for quiet beauty, to be compared with the Brazos. So much were we excited, one and all, by our prospects, that we sat up, half the night, admiring the fair moon, the bright stars, and the atmosphere without dew, conversing upon various matters of practical utility, connected with our intended settlement, and relating anecdotes we had gleaned from others, or incidents of our own experience. I wished most earnestly, that some of my northern friends, of cultivation and taste, who in their finished dwellings, far, far off—are pitying, perhaps, my singular destiny, or wondering at my adventurous hardihood, had been with me, to participate in the rare pleasure of that day. They, with their habitual foresight, are preparing their winter clothing and hoarding their winter fuel, for with them,

> "November's wind is chill and drear,"
> "November's leaf is red and sear."

Long, long may they enjoy, their Christmas fires, their Christmas cheer, and all the blessings of their happy, happy lot.

Affectionately, yours, &c.

LETTER IV.

Bolivar, Texas, December, 1831.

THE shores of the Brazos are not flat, though never bold, but undulating and graceful. The prairies, only are level, gently sloping towards the bay. The trees of larger growth are some-times covered with Spanish moss, as on the shores of the Mississippi. But these bearded non-de-scripts are not so frequent as to give the sensation of gloom; nor is there any cypress, to increase that effect on the mind. Where the land is of, comparatively, recent formation, the growth is of willow and cotton wood, with occasional young sycamores; but this is not very frequent. The Brazos pursues the noiseless tenour of its way, and never overflows its banks, in its whole course, of many hundred miles. In colour, it is more red than the Mississippi or the Missouri, and resembles that of Red river. From the centre, both shores show to advantage. There is no caving in, no *cut offs*, no dead timber, and scarcely a snag. Nature in its solitudes, is quiet

and lovely, and subject, here, to no violence.
Such, at least, was its aspect, when I saw it. I
have been informed, it is not always so. In the
common stage of water, it is justly represented
by images of gentleness and peace. The water
is, then, tranquil, and its onward movement, silent
and uniform. Where it is seldom disturbed, as
above Brazoria, it is as smooth as a mirror,
slightly tinged with green. I am told, indeed,
that all the rivers of Texas, when undisturbed by
freshets, have this greenish hue, like the sea in
shallow water.

When, on the contrary, the mountain torrents,
pour down, with their infusions of red clay, the
Brazos becomes dark and furious, tearing away
all obstructions of its channel, but never carrying
away its banks. In its former state, it may be
compared, in tranquillity, to a lamb: in the latter,
to a roaring lion, foaming with blood.

Thus its name, "El Brazos de Dios," is sig-
nificant of its character; being placid and benefi-
cent in repose—mighty and terrible in wrath.

We saw but one alligator. These creatures
are lazy and harmless, and not ferocious, devour-
ing animals, as some suppose. You must tread
on them, as they lie basking in the sun, before

they will move, and then, they slowly drag their
clumsy length along. This one was fired at, and
twice hit, without stirring, and a billet of wood,
at last, drove him into his natural element. We
were near to him, and closely inspected his ugly
proportions. Never was such odious deformity.

We have not been, at all, incommoded by
mosquetos, or other insects, during this voyage,
and have, but two nights, made use of mosqueto
bars.

We reached Brazoria on the evening of the
26th, being the third day from the mouth of the
river, and the sixth, from New Orleans. Thus,
had we not been detained by the bar, and by
getting aground, we should have made the whole
passage in four days. The last ten miles, we had
to *warp*, as the sailors term it, the turns were so
numerous, and the wind so fitful and faint. It
certainly cannot be long, before all tedious delays
from this cause, will be remedied by the interposition of steam power. Never, was a river
better calculated than the Brazos, whether we
consider its depth, its placid current, or unob-
structed channel, for the perfect operation of the
steam engine. At present, they say, there is not
enough of business to defray the expense of a

steamboat. The experiment has been made. But
the tide of population is setting in so strongly and
trade increasing so rapidly, that this objection,
must of course, be speedily removed.

Some of the passengers, tired of confinement,
went ashore, to exercise their limbs and survey
the land. They proceeded to town on foot, and
arrived there long before us. They saw many
deer, in their walk. They, with the male population, en masse, stood on the shore, the future
quay, to welcome us. An arrival at Brazoria, is
an event of some moment; and the schooner
Spica excited a far livelier interest than the Lady
Clinton or the Benjamin Franklin usually do in
the docks of New York and Boston. The *port*
was not crowded with shipping, nor would it be
slander to allude to *grass-grown* streets. We
were safely moored among tall masts (the only
masts there) still flourishing in all their leafy
honors. Not a *naked spar*, save ours, was to be
seen, nor an inch of canvass, to dispute the su-
premacy of nature over art.

The staging being adjusted, we were soon
boarded, not by Spanish myrmidons, or cannibal
Indians, but by friends and kinsmen, all of the
same complexion with ourselves, and speaking

our native tongue. The letter bag was the first object of curiosity, and its interesting contents were soon searched.

Too much must not be expected of Brazoria. It is not located in a prairie, where nothing was to be done to prepare the foundation of the rising city, but to mark off its lines with compass and chain; but upon a wooded elevation of peach-land, as it is called. This spot was chosen as the most commanding and healthful, besides combining other advantages. It has, therefore, to dispute empire with the lords of the forest, which are paying tribute to the power of man, in every possible position, from the erect to the prostrate. One street stretches along the bank of the Brazos, and one parallel with it farther back, while other streets, with the trees still standing, are laid out to intersect these at right angles, to be cleared at some future day, as the wants of the citizens may require. Its arrangements, as well as its wealth and greatness, are all prospective. A speedy settlement and a rapid growth in population and importance, are calculated upon with perfect certainty. Nor will these calculations appear unreasonable, when we consider that it is but three years since the first tree was cut, and it now

4

contains fifty families, many of which are of the
first respectability. A stranger is more surprised
to see brick stores and frame dwelling houses,
than disposed to complain that he does not find
more elegance and convenience.

Brazoria gives constant employment to the
few carpenters there, so many buildings are required by the rapid increase of population from
abroad. Every body here is employed, and
every house occupied. Some families, recently
arrived, are obliged to *camp out*, from the im-
practicability of getting other accommodation.
The place has, therefore, a busy and prosperous
air, which it is always agreeable to notice, but
has not yet advanced beyond the wants of first
necessity. There is neither cabinet-maker,
tailor, hatter, shoe-maker, nor any other me-
chanic, except carpenters above mentioned, not
even a blacksmith. Such persons would, of
course, find encouragement and business. By
combining agriculture with their trade, they need
not fear a want of employment. The useful arts
only are likely to be encouraged in a new colony.
Sound policy, indeed, should teach the colonists
to look coldly on whatever tends to extravagance
of any kind.

Brazoria is thirty miles from the mouth of the Brazos by the meanders of the river, and fifteen by land. It is situated on the right bank, and contains from two to three hundred inhabitants. It has a very good boarding-house, that is, one that furnishes every thing that absolute necessity requires, in neatness and good order. The proprietors of it are from New York, and know how things should be, and have intelligence and good sense enough to make the best of circumstances they cannot control. Thus they contrive to render their house, not only a comfortable, but an agreeable sojourn for travellers. A hotel is about to be erected, which will accommodate a greater number of persons. It is a very desirable thing to have such a one here, as in all places, the first impression, whether favourable or the contrary, depends so much upon the degree of personal comfort enjoyed.

Brazoria has, already, some families of education and refinement. In one of my visiting excursions, I called on Mrs. ———, who was, I found, from my native state, (Connecticut,) a circumstance sufficient to place us, at once, on the most sociable footing. The family had not been here long, and their *cabin* was not yet built.

They occupied a temporary shed among the trees, or *camp*, as they call it here, not impervious to the light, though there was no window. A white curtain supplied the place of door. The single apartment contained three or four beds, as white as snow. Books, glass, china, and other furniture in polite usage, were arranged in perfect neatness about the room, as best suited the present exigence. It was Sunday evening. Mrs. ———— was seated in a white cambric wrapper and tasteful cap. The children around the door, and the servants, were at their several occupations, or sitting at leisure about the temporary fire-place without. The whole scene was an exhibition of peace and happiness. I gazed upon it with emotions of admiration and delight. I have seldom seen a more striking domestic group, or enjoyed a conversation of more genuine good sense, than during the hour of my visit. The prospects of a new country and the retrospect of the old, were of course the absorbing topics of our discourse, as they are the unfailing themes of conversation among all classes in Brazoria, all uniting to extol the advantages of these fair regions of the sun, over the frozen climates of the north. Mr. ———— is an alumnus of Yale College. Stimulated by the love of occupation and the desire of doing good, he is about to open a school, in which the higher branches of education will be taught; the first school in Brazoria.

Nowhere is conversation so animated as here, where every body is excited by the beautiful creations around them, and all busily engaged in appropriating the luxuriant bounties of heaven to their own use. Each has the best land, the best water courses, the finest timber, and the most judicious mode of operation; proving, at least, that each is satisfied with his own lot, and not disposed to envy his neighbour. Never was self more amiably displayed. Never was rivalry more honourable in itself, or one that promised more beneficial results to the community.

In Texas, most domestic business is transacted in the open air. There has not been time to attend to the supernumerary wants of convenient kitchens. The most simple process is used for culinary purposes, and one is often reminded that hands were made before tongs, shovel and poker, as well as before knives and forks. Rumford and Franklin seem to have laboured in vain, and the amusing melody of mother Goose is almost

4*

realised; for pots, kettles, and frying-pans, in playful confusion, greet the eyes of visiters and enjoy the benefit of fresh air, as well as of severe scrutiny.

Affectionately, yours, &c.

LETTER V.

Bolivar, Texas, December, 1831.

FREQUENT mention was made, in conversation, of *honey trees.* In Kentucky, you hear of *sugar trees.* Upon inquiring what kind of tree was meant by honey tree, I learned, that hollow trees, in which the bees deposit their honey, are so called. These trees are very abundant, and honey of excellent quality and in any quantity, may be obtained from them. These trees are also called *bee trees.* There are persons here, who have a peculiar tact in coursing the bee, and of thus discovering these deposits of the luscious store. This employment is not a mere pastime, but is profitable. The wax alone, thus obtained, is a valuable article of commerce in Mexico, and commands a high price. There is always a demand for it, it is so much used in the churches. This, it will be remembered, is a Catholic country. In some of the churches, the wax candles made use of, are as large as a man's arm. It often happens, that the hunters throw away the honey, and save only the wax.

The character of Leather Stocking, is not uncommon in Texas. Many persons employ an individual in the business of hunting, in all its branches; and thus, are constantly supplied with provisions of every description, even to eggs, which are furnished by the immense numbers of wild fowl. These hunters are very profitable to their employers, and much cherished in the family, and often become spoiled by familiarity and indulgence. A roughness of manners, and a rudeness of speech are tolerated in them, which would not be brooked in other servants. They are a sort of privileged character. Indians and Mexicans, are considered the best qualified for this important office. But it sometimes happens that a white man from the *States*, who has become somewhat de-civilized, (to coin a word,) is substituted. The dress of these hunters is usually of deer-skin. Hence the appropriate name *Leather Stocking.* Their generic name, for they form a distinct class, is *Frontiers-men.*

Mr. McNeal employs an Indian hunter. His table is always supplied with venison and other game. This gentleman came to Texas four years since. He brought with him six sons, and twenty negroes. With this force he opened a cotton plantation, from which he already realizes an annual income of ten thousand dollars. His plantation is below Brazoria, ten miles from the Gulf, which, with every passing sail, it over-looks. A prairie only, intervenes. A situation more beautiful cannot be found.

It is a very curious fact, in the natural history of the bee, that it is never found in a wild coun-try, but always precedes civilization, forming a kind of advance guard between the white man and the savage. The Indians, at least, are per-fectly convinced of the truth of this fact, for it is a common remark among them, when they observe these happy insects, "there come the white men."

The people of Texas should take the bee for their emblem, as the Mexican nation has done the Cactus, Nopal, or Prickly Pear; and for the same reason, its abundance and delicious fruits. For their motto, I would add, this most appropriate sentiment: "Industry is Fortune's right hand."

The Nopal, or Prickly Pear, which you may observe in the Mexican coat of arms, is a very interesting and valuable production of Mexico. In some districts of the upper country, it grows in great abundance, and forms, in places impenetrable thickets, higher than a man on horseback. This plant produces an immense quantity of fruit, which, together with the young leaves, furnishes food for vast herds of cattle and wild horses. On this account, the Mexicans, when selecting land for a stock farm, always choose that which has a good proportion of the Nopal.

Of the fruit of the Nopal, there are two kinds; one is a scarlet, about the size and shape of a large pear. The other is much longer, and, when ripe, of a yellowish white color. The latter is most esteemed, and is sold in the market of Mexico as a choice fruit.

During the revolution, the army of the patriots was, at one time, preserved from famine by the fruit of the Nopal. Which circumstance, in connexion with its never-failing abundance, its great value for feeding cattle, and for nourishing the Cochineal Insect, probably suggested the idea of adopting it as a part of the Mexican Arms.

Among the superstitions of the Mexicans, there is a tradition, from which many credulous people derive the origin of this emblem. The Mexicans, it is said, originally inhabited a cold climate, and a barren, mountainous country, where, with difficulty, they gathered a scanty subsistence. They resolved to migrate in a body. The Great Spirit appeared to the king in a vision, and directed him to lead his nation to the south. An eagle should fly before them to direct their course. This guide they were to follow, until it should settle and finally disappear.

In conformity with these instructions, the whole nation followed the eagle, which according to promise, flew before them. The eagle stopped on a tree in California, but did not disappear, continuing to fly around and around the same spot, every day. The king, believing that this was the place destined for the permanent location of his people, caused large storehouses to be erected, the ruins of which may be seen in the forests of California to this day, known by the name of "las casas grandes."

At this place the nation remained a few years, the eagle still hovering round the spot. At length the king received an indication, by means of another vision, that the eagle would lead them to their permanent home, having rested at that place only to let them recruit. Accordingly, the winged guide again set his feathered sails for the destined haven. The nation, with the king at their head, again followed the eagle, until he settled upon a Nopal, on an island in the lake Tescuco, and shortly afterwards, died. This was pronounced by the king, priests, and wise men of the nation, to be the spot designed by the Great Spirit, for their permanent location. Here they remained and founded the city of Mexico.

From Brazoria to Bolivar, I came in a sailboat, with occasional rowing, as the wind subsided or was unfavourable. The weather was fine, and the scenery picturesque. The different reaches of the river, resembling so many lakes in a chain, were like mirrors, to reflect from their polished surfaces, the shores of unbroken forests. The limpid water, instead of being muddy and red, as below Brazoria, looked as if it passed over a bed of emeralds, and had not been disturbed since creation. No human creature was to be seen, and the numerous flocks of birds were so tame, as seemingly to court our acquaintance. A basking alligator and an occasional herd of cattle, which gazed at us with almost human curiosity, were the only objects which interrupted our musings. A solitude more complete, it is not easy to imagine. But I enjoyed it. The universal repose of nature inspired my heart with solemn, peaceful, pleasing emotions.

Half way between Brazoria and Bolivar, is the town of Marion, or Bell's Landing, from the name of the proprietor. It has two or three cabins, a country store, and one frame house painted white. The lofty forest trees have been left standing, in sufficient numbers to protect it from the vertical sun, and to prevent the banks from sinking. This little village, as I strolled among its quiet shades at noon, struck my fancy very agreeably. You must know, it is the common practice with settlers here, to cut away every tree of a clearing, and to substitute, for the noble giants of the forest, those of diminutive size, and ephemeral growth; whether with a view to shade or ornament, I know not; but it certainly is a very mistaken policy, as well as most wretched taste. Fine trees are not the growth of a life-time. How much better is it to suffer those to live, which are venerable by age and size, which, by their elevation do not obstruct the free circulation of air nor harbour insects; but, being trimmed to the top, serve as true parasols to the dwellings they ornament.

How would Europeans be astonished to be told that almost every settler in Texas, hews or burns down the fine live oaks that grow about his door, and thus, in this sunny climate, leaves his roof without a shelter from the rays of the sun.

Before sun-set, I arrived at this my forest home, for such Bolivar may now be regarded, being the place of my temporary abode in Texas. Bolivar, though selected as an advantageous location for a commercial town, and laid off for that purpose before Brazoria, at present consists of but a single residence. Its location, for purposes of trade as well as on account of the fertility of the adjacent country, has doubtless many advantages. But it was abandoned for that which was regarded, upon the whole, as a more eligible position, on account of its easier access from the sea. It is at the head of tide water on the Brazos, sixty miles from the river's mouth by

5

water and forty-five by land.   It is an important point, as any vessel that can pass the bar can ascend to this place in the lowest stage of water, but not farther.   It is fifteen miles nearer to San Felipe than Brazoria, and the road much better. The distance from Bolivar to the navigable waters of the Galveston bay, is but fifteen miles, over a high, dry prairie, with the exception of six miles through timber land, where the road is now good.

The land, in and about Bolivar, is the best in the colony; clothed with heavy timber, with peach and cane undergrowth, to the distance of six miles from the river.   The bank of the river in front of the town, is a high bluff of stiff red clay.   About fifty acres are cleared and under cultivation.

The undergrowth of the best land in the Brazos valley, is cane and a species of laurel, the leaves of which taste like the kernel of the peach stone, containing an extraordinary quantity of prussic acid.   The leaves resemble those of the peach tree.   Hence it is called by the colonists, wild peach.   This tree is an evergreen and grows to the height of twenty or thirty feet, though its usual height does not exceed ten feet.

This tree is regarded as a certain indication of
the best soil. Hence, when a colonist wishes to
describe his land as first rate, he says it is all
peach and cane land.

Affectionately, yours, &c.

————

LETTER VI.

Bolivar, Texas, December, 1831.

I have now been domiciliated at this place for
some weeks. The interval has passed away
very delightfully, and I trust, not without im-
provement. I have been greatly interested in
every thing I have seen and heard relative to the
country, and though my anticipations respecting
it were sufficiently sanguine, I do assure you they
have not been disappointed. I have been fortunate in enjoying the conversation of some of the
oldest colonists and most intelligent men of the
country, from whom I have gathered much valuable information respecting the history and geography of Texas. From copious notes taken at

the moment, I now proceed to give you the result of my inquiries. These inquiries relate to the general face of the country, including its rivers, soil, productions, towns, and harbours; Indians, climate, and natural resources; the history of its original settlement, together with the present condition and encouragements of colonization.

I shall endeavour to be as systematic in my remarks as I can, but you must not expect the complete and formal arrangement of a book.

Texas at present forms a part of the state of Coahuila and Texas, being provisionally annexed to Coahuila, until its population and resources are sufficient to form a separate State, when its connexion with Coahuila will be dissolved. Its latitude is, from 28° to 34° north, and is bounded by Louisiana on the east, by Red river, which divides it from Arkansas, on the north, by the Nueces river, which divides it from Tamaulipas and Coahuila, on the west, and by the Gulf of Mexico on the south.

Texas is divided into three distinct tracts or regions, whose characteristics are, in many respects, entirely different. These are, the *level*, the *undulating*, and the *mountainous* or *hilly*.

The whole coast, from the Sabine river to the Neuces, is rather low and very level, but entirely free from marsh; so much so, that in most places a loaded wagon may be driven to the beach without obstruction. There is a belt of prairie along its whole coast, about eight or ten miles wide. This prairie is destitute of timber, except narrow skirts, on the margins of the rivers and creeks.

That part of the level region which lies between the Sabine and San Jacinto rivers, extends back about seventy miles from the coast, in a north and north-westerly direction. This tract is, in general, heavily timbered with pine, oak, ash, cedar, cypress, and other forest trees. The Sabine, Naches, and Trinity rivers, are all navigable entirely through this section, and the latter for a considerable distance above it. The Naches affords good navigation to the junction of the Angelina, twenty-five miles south-east of Nacogdoches.

North and north-west of this section of the level region, the country is undulating to Red river; there being no portion of it sufficiently broken to be called hilly. The thickly timbered or wooded lands, extend quite to Red river, and

5*

as far west, as a line drawn due north from the heads of the Sabine. West of this line, there is a wide belt of undulating prairie, extending along Red river, which is thinly timbered, the timber being confined to the margins of the streams.

The whole of this eastern section of Texas is very well watered by the above mentioned rivers and their tributaries, which afford many favourable sites for saw-mills and manufactories. The soil, in general, is well adapted to agriculture and grazing. The timber business, from this quarter, will become very valuable, for the supply of the southern ports of the Gulf of Mexico, as soon as mills are put into extensive operation. One steam saw-mill is already completed at Harrisburg, and another will soon be in operation on the east bank of the San Jacinto, opposite the mouth of Buffalo Bayou.

The old Spanish military post and village of Nacogdoches, is situated in this eastern section of Texas, in latitude 31° 40', sixty miles west of the Sabine river. In 1819 or 1820, it was totally broken up by the revolution and abandoned. Its inhabitants were driven away by the Spanish troops and compelled to seek a refuge in Louisiana, near Nachitoches, exiles from their native country, and dependent in most instances, on the hospitality of strangers.

Nacogdoches remained without population, until the year 1822–23, when many of the emigrants who left the United States with the view of joining Austin's Colony, stopped at this place. A number of the ancient inhabitants, also, returned to their former possessions, and thus the town has been gradually re-peopled and is now a respectable village. A garrison of Mexican troops is stationed here under the command of a Colonel of the army. There is, also, a custom house establishment, for the collection of duties on the inland trade from Louisiana. The country on the road between this place and the Sabine, is thinly settled by emigrants from the United States.

A military post and town has been established by order of General Teran, on the north-east corner of Galveston bay, opposite the mouth of Trinity river, called *Anahuac*. The lands on Trinity river and the lands on the lower portion of the Naches, is pretty well settled. There is a settlement of about two hundred and fifty families on Red river, above the mouth of Sul-

phur fork, which, it is supposed, will fall within
the boundary of Texas when the line is accu-
rately run.

The section of the level region ıying between the San Jacinto and Guadalupe rivers, including the lower parts of the Brazos, San Bernard, Colorado, and La Baca rivers, extends into
the interior about eighty miles from the coast, in
a northerly direction. This beautiful and very
valuable portion of Texas as far as the La Baca,
is embraced in Austin's Colony. The land is sufficiently elevated to drain easily and rapidly after
heavy rains. It is entirely clear of all marsh,
lakes, and overflow. The supply of pure water
is sufficiently abundant in the rivers and creeks,
while excellent water for domestic purposes may
be obtained from wells, at a moderate depth, in
every part of this territory.

The alluvial bottom lands of the Brazos, San
Bernard, and Colorado, are from three to twenty
miles in width. They are heavily timbered with
live oak, with red, black, and other species of
oak, with cedar, pecan, elm, hackberry, mulberry, and all the other varieties of forest trees
and undergrowth common in the rich alluvions
of the Mississippi. The cane-brakes are of im-

mense extent, particularly on Cane-brake creek. On this creek there is an uninterrupted cane-brake seventy-five miles long and from one to three miles wide. It extends on both sides of the creek, from within twelve miles of its mouth into the gulf, to its source, a few hundred yards from the Colorado river. Scarcely a tree is to be found in this ocean of cane, which has, hence, received the name of the Great Prairie Cane-brake. It is bordered on each side by the heavy and lofty timber of the alluvial soils.

Cane-brake creek or *Caney*, as it is usually called, winds its way through this tract, and exhibits so many and such unequivocal evidences of its having been once a branch of the Colorado river, that not a reasonable doubt exists that such is the fact. The bed of the creek is of equal depth and of equal width, with the bed of the river. The appearance of the banks, the nature of the adjacent soil, in short, every feature is the same in both. What seems to confirm the above suggestion beyond controversy, is the abrupt termination of the deep, wide bed of Caney, within less than two hundred yards of the bank of the river, in an alluvial bottom nearly ten miles in width. From these appearances, it is very evident that the Colorado, at some former period, divided at or near the present source of Caney and discharged its waters into the gulf by two distinct mouths more than twenty-five miles apart, forming an extensive island. This island constituted what is now called the Bay Prairie; a large, rich, and very beautiful prairie, lying between the timbered lands of Caney, and those of the Colorado. Not any of the water of the river has been known to flow into Caney since Austin's colony was commenced, nor is there any indication of there having been an overflow for many years.

Oyster creek, on the east side of the Brazos river, affords also extensive bodies of prairie cane-brake, though by no means so extensive as that which has just been mentioned. The cane land on Oyster creek extends indeed along its entire course, but it is not all prairie cane-brake, in many places being interspersed with heavy timber. This singular creek takes its rise in the alluvial lands of the Brazos. Winding its course through the bottoms of this river, which it drains, it discharges into the gulf two miles east of its mouth. Oyster creek forms a connexion with the Brazos at Bolivar, by a deep channel, through which the waters of the river, in time of freshets, pour their crimson tide with a rapid current.

The soil of the Brazos, Bernard, Caney, and Colorado lands, has the same general character, as to appearance, fertility, and natural productions. It is of a reddish cast, nearly resembling a chocolate colour, and is evidently alluvial, formed by deposits of the rivers during freshets. The colour of the soil is precisely such as would be expected from the appearance of the river at such seasons: for the Brazos and Colorado, when swollen by the spring and autumn freshets, are of a deep red and very turbid. The deposits from these rivers at these stages, are very great; much greater than that from the waters of either the Mississippi or Red river.

The beds of these rivers are deep and narrow. Their banks are clayey and not so liable to wear away as sandy banks, nor easily permit a change of channel.

The Guadalupe, La Baca, Navidad, and a great number of fine rivulets that intersect this level region, also afford valuable bottoms of rich alluvial black soil, all of which are well clothed with timber.

These alluvions are in the highest degree productive and easily cultivated. Three thousand pounds of seed cotton and seventy-five bushels of Indian corn or maize, are an average crop in these lands.

That remarkable feature of the Brazos river, the Salt Branch, has been already mentioned. It is probably owing to this peculiarity that the land of the Brazos has a fertility so truly extraordinary. The freshets of the fresh branches are much more copious and frequent than those of the Salt Branch. They all rise and flow through very rich land, and their waters go towards the sea, charged with fine loam and clay washed into them by the floods.

The alternate deposits by these salt and fresh tributaries in time of freshets, form a soil of a light reddish brown colour, slightly impregnated with salt and nitre. The colour of the water varies from a deep red to almost chocolate, according as the one or the other rise prevails. Salt and saltpetre, it is well known, are potent manures. This bright *mulatto* soil, as it is called, formed in this manner, is considered the best land in Texas. The whole valley of the Brazos is mostly of this description. On the surface of this alluvion, a black mould is formed by the decomposition of vegetable matter. The soil, properly speaking, possessing the power of vegetation in all its vigour, extends to an unlimited depth. When brought to the surface from a depth of twenty feet, it will produce as good crops as the surface itself.

Where this mulatto soil is found, the banks of the rivers and smaller streams are clothed with heavy timber. Near the sea coast, the timber is mostly live oak of enormous size, intermixed with Spanish oak, red and black oak, ash, sycamore, mulberry, pecan, hackberry, and other kinds. Immediately on the bank of the river cotton wood abounds. At Bolivar, the timber tract is five or six miles wide and the road to the prairie is walled in with tall cane filling all the space between the trees.

The live oak region is from the Bay of Matagorda to the west end of Galveston bay, and extends on the banks of the Brazos towards the interior about seventy miles. There is a live oak tree in Bolivar, sixteen feet in circumference, and keeps this size more than thirty feet from the ground. It then spreads out its enormous branches. Larger trees than this, however, are

6

not uncommon. Ten miles from Bolivar, there is a tree which measures nineteen feet in circumference. What would such trees be worth in the dock yards of the United States or of England!

About fifteen miles east of the Brazos, the live oak region ends. Thence to the Sabine river, fine cedar, Spanish oak, post and red oak, and black oak, ash and mulberry, with other common timbers, are the growth on the water courses.

The intervening country between the rivers, creeks, and rivulets, is open, level, rich, and elevated prairie, clothed with a thick and luxuriant growth of grass of a good quality for pasturage, with occasional *points* and *islands* of timber, as the wooded projections and scattered clumps of trees are called, which give the plains the appearance of vast parks, with ornamental trees artificially arranged to beautify the prospect. Nothing can exceed the beauty of these vast, natural meadows in the spring and summer seasons; neither is it possible to form an estimate, even in imagination, of the number of useful domestic animals that may be reared on them without trouble or expense. Even in the winter season, the pasturage is sufficiently good to dispense with feeding live stock.

The value of the prairie lands is not confined, however, to grazing alone. These lands are so nearly equal to timbered alluvions for all the purposes of planting and farming, that many persons who have cultivated this kind of land, prefer it to the alluvial bottoms. They maintain that the prairie, when properly broken up by the plough and sufficiently mellowed, will yield crops nearly equal to the best alluvions. That the labour, expense, and time, required to clear twenty acres of timbered bottom land and prepare it for cultivation, would be sufficient to prepare sixty acres of prairie; that, supposing both kinds of land to be equally prepared, a hand can cultivate two-thirds more of the latter than of the former. So that, taking all things into account, the cultivation of the prairie land requires less capital in the outset and is more profitable in the end, than the cultivation of the bottoms. Experience has proved that these calculations are not unfounded, and that the prairies are valuable for all the purposes of farming, as well as for grazing. The soil of the prairies is a deep black mould mixed with sand in various proportions.

Of the settlements in this region of country, besides Brazoria, which has been already mentioned, a town has been laid off at the mouth of the Colorado river, on the bay of Matagorda, called Matagorda. This place must become the depot of the Colorado river and of an extensive fertile country which will find its natural market at this point.

The town of San Felipe de Austin was founded in 1824, by Col. Austin and the commissioner of the government, Baron de Bastrop. It is the capital of Austin's Colony, situated on the right bank of the Brazos river, eighty miles from the gulf by land, and one hundred and eighty miles by the meanders of the river. The site of this town is exceedingly beautiful. It is a high prairie bluff, which strikes the river at the upper or northern limit of the level region. It is the residence of the Empresario, Col. Austin. The state and municipal officers of the jurisdiction hold their offices here, and here all the land and judicial business of the colony is transacted.

Above the level region just noticed, upon the Brazos, Colorado, and Guadalupe rivers, the country becomes gently and beautifully undulating. This description of land extends in a north-west direction up those rivers, from one hundred and fifty to two hundred miles above the level region, and reaches to the mountain range of Texas. This extensive undulating section is probably as desirable a country for the residence of man, as any other on the face of the earth. Whether we regard productiveness of soil, healthfulness of climate, or beauty of natural landscape, it cannot be surpassed. The soil, in general, is of the first quality of black mould, easily cultivated and very productive. The climate is much more healthful and pleasant than that of the level region. There are no mosquetos and very few insects of any kind. The surface is beautifully and often fancifully diversified with prairie and woodland, presenting to the enterprising farmer, large and fertile fields already cleared by the hand of nature, and waiting, as it were, to receive the plough. The woods which encircle the prairies, afford the best of oak, cedar, ash, and other timber, valuable for fencing and building.

The whole of this undulating region, is most bountifully watered, and abounds in bold rivulets and springs of pure water. These rivulets have all more or less of bottom land adjacent to them

6*

and are lined with the lofty forest trees of the
rich alluvions.

The undulations, in many places, rise into eminences of considerable elevation, but always with
a gentle ascent and with lengthened intervals.
Abrupt elevations or cliffs seldom occur, nor is
the surface so uneven or broken, as to be justly
designated hilly. From the summit of these elevations the view is extensive and imposing.
The landscape is rich and splendid, and the eye
delights to roam over the smooth, verdant, extended slopes. The round tops of the eminences
are here crowned with tufts of cedars or groves of
oaks and pecans; there presenting an unbroken
surface of grass. The pale green of the prairie
sprinkled with flowers of every hue, forms a
pleasing contrast with the dark foliage of the cedars and other lofty forest trees: while the rivulets which wind their serpentine course at the
foot of the undulations, agreeably diversify the
scene. All combined under a clear blue sky,
present a picture, not only delightful to the eye
but enchanting to the imagination, which, with
the pencil of fancy, would fain fill up the scene
under view, with rural cottages, with the flocks

of the herdsman, and all the various indications
of human activity and domestic happiness.

Successful experiments have been made in various places on these undulating lands, of wheat,
rye, oats, and flax, and the result satisfactorily
establishes the fact, that these articles may be
cultivated upon them to any extent. All the
fruits and agricultural productions of the level
region arrive at perfection here, except sugar and
Sea Island cotton. It is considered to be fully
equal to the level region, for raising black cattle
and hogs, and far superior to it for rearing horses
and sheep. Lime stone and building stone of various sorts may be obtained in any abundance in
this tract, neither of which has yet been discovered in the level country. Indigenous grapes,
of several varieties, grow in great profusion, and
extensive natural vineyards await the hand of the
vine-dresser.

A military post and town has been established
on the right bank of the Brazos, twelve miles
above the upper road leading from Bexar to
Nacogdoches, fifteen miles below the mouth of
the San Andress river, and one hundred miles
above San Felipe de Austin. This post is called
Tenoxticlan. It is very eligibly situated and

abundantly supplied with excellent water. It is the intention of the government to keep a garrison at this place, for the twofold purpose of protecting the frontiers of Austin's Colony from the predatory incursions of Indians, and of facilitating the extension of that colony, northwesterly, up the Brazos river. The adjacent country for many miles around, is fertile and heathful, and the Brazos in seasons of freshets, is navigable some miles above this port.

A new town is about to be established by the Empresario, Col. Austin, in his contract of 1827, on the left bank of the Colorado, at the intersection of the road above mentioned, with the river. An abundant supply of fine cedar, oak, ash, and other timber is found at this spot, as also lime and other building stone, clay and sand suitable for brick-making.

The town of Gonzales, the capital of De Witt's Colony, is situated in the tract of country now under review. It is on the left bank of the Guadalupe river, at the point where the direct road from San Felipe de Austin intersects that river. The site of this town is elevated, pleasant, and healthful, and possesses many natural advantages.

To return to the level or coast lands. That portion of them which lies to the west and south-west of the Guadalupe, lying between that river and the Neuces, differs in some important respects from that which stretches to the eastward, and which has been already noticed. This tract is much narrower than the eastern tract and not so well clothed with timber. The distance from the bay shore to the undulating lands varies from twenty-five to thirty miles. The margins of the Aransaso and Neuces bays are also much higher than the margins of the bays lying farther eastward. The whole tract is more elevated, though level, than any parts of the level regions before noticed. The climate also, is believed to be more salubrious and pleasant. The soil of this tract, like that of the other prairie lands, is a deep black mould, very fertile and productive. The pasturage here, is confessed to be even superior to that of any other district of the country, consisting of a different species of grass, called Muskit grass, (pronounced Muskeet.) This grass bears a strong resemblance to the blue grass, so common in the United States, and furnishes the most nutritious pasturage. It continues green throughout the winter, and retains its nutritious qualities, even after it has become dry and apparently dead.

The Muskìt tree also abounds here, affording excellent fire-wood and valuable materials for fencing; while forests of oak, ash, and other timber suitable for building, flourish on the margins of the water courses.

Two Irish gentlemen have contracted with the government to settle an Irish colony on this tract.   The boundaries of the contemplated colony embrace all the lands between the Guadalupe and Neuces rivers, within ten leagues of the gulf or bay shore.   This is a very valuable part of Texas, and there can be no doubt but that many thousands of the oppressed sons of Erin, if they possessed the information and means of emigration, would joyfully exchange their "cows grass" and "potatoe lots" for rich farms in this colony.   Here are no tithes, no poor rates, no burthensome exactions, nor vexatious restrictions. Here enterprize and energy may unfold themselves to their fullest extent, in all the various pursuits of honest industry, without fear and without reproach.   The colony has already commenced operations under favourable auspices, and will doubtless succeed and ultimately flourish.

Nothing is now wanting to insure its immediate success, but a sufficient supply of industrious emigrants.

The undulating region succeeds to the level tracts just noticed, between the Guadalupe and Neuces, which, stretching in a north-westerly direction and gradually increasing in elevation, finally terminates in the mountain range, a distance of about two hundred miles. The whole of this extensive tract affords the best of pasturage, being principally clothed with the Muskìt grass, and is, on this account, peculiarly adapted to grazing and the raising of stock of every description. Timber and water are not, however, so abundant as in the country lying farther east. The Nopal thrives here with greatest luxuriance, forming oftentimes impenetrable thickets, and furnishing, with its fruit and leaves, a bountiful supply of excellent food for cattle and wild horses.

The Muskìt tree before mentioned, the most common tree found in this section, is a species of locust. Its size is about that of a peach tree, which, when viewed at a distance, it very much resembles in appearance. The leaves of it are similar to those of the honey locust, but much

smaller. It bears a pod about the size and shape
of the common snap bean, quite sweet to the
taste, and when dry, is used by the Indians in
times of scarcity, for food. It is highly valued
by the Mexicans, who maintain, that for purposes
of fattening cattle and hogs, it is equal to Indian
corn. The wood of the Muskìt is very durable,
as much so as black locust or cedar, and hence
its value as a material for fencing.

Lime stone and building stone of good quality
abound, and are procured with little labour.

The ancient town of Bexar is situated in this
region of country, on the San Antonio river,
which flows through it. This place is in latitude
29° 25′, 140 miles from the coast, and contains
2500 inhabitants, all native Mexicans, with the
exception of a very few American families who
have settled there. A military out-post was established at this spot by the Spanish government
in 1718. In the year 1731, the town was settled by emigrants sent out from the Canary
Islands by the king of Spain. It became a
flourishing settlement, and so continued till the
revolution in 1812. Since which period the Co⁻
manche and other Indians have greatly harrassed
the inhabitants, producing much individual suffer-

fering, and totally destroying for a season, at least, the prosperity of the town.

All the land cultivated in this vicinity, is irrigated from the San Antonio river. To facilitate this purpose, a low dam of stone is thrown across the river, which diverts a portion of the water into a small canal leading to the cultivated grounds. More than two hundred thousand acres of land might be irrigated, at and below this place, with great ease and with trifling expense. The soil is rich, and the principal articles cultivated by the inhabitants, are corn, sugar cane, beans, and other vegetables.

This place is admirably located for the establishment of manufactories, especially of cotton and wool. The supply of water is abundant, and the fall of the river sufficient to admit the advantageous application of it to machinery, at very frequent intervals. The San Antonio seldom or never overflows its banks, nor is it exposed to sudden or violent freshets, its source being within three leagues of Bexar, and there is not sufficient space for any dangerous accumulation of water. From a concentration of innumerable springs, which unite their rivulets within a few hundred yards of their fountains, the San Antonio bursts

7

forth at once a river, and its chrystal waters flow off with a rapid current over a bed of limestone.

The village of Goliad, formerly La Bahia, is situated on the right bank of the San Antonio river, about 110 miles south-east of Bexar, and 30 miles from the coast. This place contains about 800 inhabitants, all Mexicans.

A second Irish colony has been commenced on the Neuces river. A town has been laid off upon the river's bank, called San Patrick. A number of Irish families have already established themselves here, charmed with the country, and animated with the certain prospect of plenty and independence. Never was there a more inviting asylum for Irish emigrants, than is presented by the colonies on the Neuces, and it is much to be regretted that so few of them have availed themselves of the advantages here presented to them.

The mountain range of Texas may very properly be called a spur of the Cierra Madre, (mother mountain,) which it leaves near the junction of the Rio Puerco with the Rio Bravo, and pursuing a north-easterly direction, enters Texas at the sources of the Neuces river. Thence continuing in the same direction to the head

waters of the San Saba, a branch of the Colorado,
it inclines to the east, down the San Saba, crossing the Colorado some distance below the mouth
of that river, it is finally lost in the undulating
lands of the Brazos. This range does not cross
the Brazos. The country east of this river
and upon Trinity river is gently undulating, and
in some districts quite level; this description
of surface extending the whole distance to Red
river.

Spurs of the mountain range extend south-
wardly down the rivers Madina and Guadalupe,
to the vicinity of Bexar. Spurs also extend
down the rivers Slanos and Pedernales and the
smaller western tributaries of the Colorado.
Similar spurs stretch up the Colorado, above
San Saba, to a considerable distance, and round
the head-waters of the San Andress and Bosque,
tributaries of the Brazos.

The mountains are of third and fourth magnitude in point of elevation. Those of San Saba
are much the highest. They are in many places
thickly covered with forests of oak, cedar, and
other trees, interspersed with a great variety of
shrubbery. Granite, quartz, lime-stone, and other
rocks, are common. It is believed they abound

also in mineral wealth, but they have been, yet, very imperfectly explored. Iron, lead, and mineral coal, have been found, and tradition says, that a silver mine on the San Saba was successfully wrought many years ago, but the prosecution of it was arrested by the Indians, who cut off the workmen.

Towards the head waters of the Brazos, a large mass of metal is known to exist. It is of several tons weight, and said to be worshipped by the Comanche Indians. It is malleable and bright, having little oxide or rust upon its surface. A large piece of this metal was taken to New York many years since, by way of Nachitoches, under a belief that it was platina. It is said that experiments made by chemists in that city, proved it to be pure iron in a malleable state. The existence of such a mass of metal is doubtless very remarkable. It is, however, well attested by many persons in Nachitoches and in Texas, who have been at the spot and seen it. Whether it be iron, is perhaps not so well ascertained.

Extensive valleys of rich, arable, alluvial lands, are found throughout this range, particularly upon the water courses. Most of these valley lands may be irrigated at little expense, from the numerous streams which flow through them. The sides and even the summits of the mountains are, for the most part, susceptible of cultivation. The soil is sufficiently rich, and adapted to wheat, rye, and other small grain, as well as to the vine and all the northern fruits.

This range of high land on its north-western frontier is of vast advantage to the state of Texas. It not only renders the atmosphere more salubrious, but abounding in copious fountains of limpid water, it gives rise to the numberless rivulets which, having first irrigated their own fruitful valleys, flow off with a rapid current, and unite to form the large rivers of the central and western parts of the state. These last mentioned rivers are uniformly more limpid than the rivers to the east of the Brazos.

The resources of this elevated or mountainous section are very great and valuable. At some future period, it will, in all probability, supply the whole country with grain, and afford a surplus for exportation. Fine wool will be a staple article from these high lands, which are probably as well adapted to the raising of sheep as any country in the world.

7*

North of this mountain range, and on the extreme head waters of the Brazos river, the country becomes level again, and presents to the view interminable prairies. These stretch to the north and north-west, beyond Red and Arkansaw rivers, and are finally lost in the vast ocean of prairie that terminates at the foot of the Rocky mountains.

Affectionately, yours, &c.

LETTER VII.

Bolivar, Texas, December, 1831.

You are doubtless tired enough by this time of these dry, geographical details. I can only say, by way of apology, that I have made them as concise as possible, and have not permitted my imagination to expatiate for a moment, as it was very prone to do, over the delightful scenery we have traversed. I need not repeat to you, for the hundredth time, that I am charmed with this beautiful country. Its mountains, its prairies, its forests, and its rivers, all have their charms for me. Hence it is, I suppose, that what you may regard dry geographical details, affect my mind with much of the inspiration of poetry. As I have not permitted any opportunity of gathering useful information to escape me, I have yet more details of the same kind in store, with which I shall now proceed to tax your patience. You must accompany me in a trip along the coast, and take a view of the bays and inlets which indent the shores of Texas.

The following account of the harbours and bays of Texas was received, not from a landsman, but from an old sailor, who has traversed the ocean around and across in every direction. A more experienced navigator, or more accurate observer is not to be found. A spirit of enterprise in the prosecution of his profession, led him in one of his expeditions, to examine a portion of this coast; so that he speaks from actual personal observation and survey, of most of the points here noticed.

Beginning at the eastern extremity of the coast, the first large body of water is Sabine lake. The inlet into this lake has six feet of water. It is, however, difficult to cross, owing to

the mud and oyster banks which extend opposite
to this inlet, out of sight of land.

Galveston is the next inlet to the westward.
This inlet has twelve feet of water on the bar.
The harbour lies between Galveston and Pelican
islands, in which there is good anchorage in five
fathoms of water, with muddy bottom. From
the harbour, through Galveston bay, to the mouth
of Trinity river, or the San Jacinto, the navigation is difficult, being obstructed by Red Fish
bar. This bar has five feet of water at high
tides, but in northerly winds, not more than three
feet. The bay generally has about nine or ten
feet of water.

A western arm of this bay stretches to the
south-westward, along the coast, to within two
miles and a half of the Brazos river, and might
be very easily connected with that river by a
short canal. There is also an inlet at the west
end of Galveston island, which may be advan-
tageously used by small vessels, drawing not
more than six or seven feet.

An eastern arm of Galveston bay extends
along the coast, called East bay; from the head
of which there is a deep tide water creek, which
nearly intersects a similar creek from Sabine

lake. By uniting these two creeks, which might be effected with little expense, a canal communication could be opened between the bay and the lake.

The Trinity and San Jacinto rivers discharge their waters into Galveston bay. The former in the north-east, the latter in the north-west corner of it. Trinity river is navigable in time of freshets, a considerable distance above the upper road, heretofore mentioned in these letters. The San Jacinto forms a very beautiful bay at its mouth, and is navigable for any vessel that can pass Red Fish bar, as far as the mouth of Buffalo Bayou. The Buffalo Bayou is also navigable to its forks above Harrisburg, to within forty miles of San Felipe de Austin, which interval is a level prairie. It resembles a wide canal, with high and heavily timbered banks. The tide flows up as far as the forks above mentioned.

The Brazos river presents the next inlet. This river has been already noticed in part, but deserves a more particular description in this connexion. The ordinary depth of water upon the bar of this river is six feet. The bar is narrow, formed by a bank of sand not more than twenty yards wide. The harbour inside the bar

is perfectly safe, and the river is sufficiently deep
for large ships as far as Brazoria. The anchorage off this bar is good in northers, which blow
off shore, or in light southerly winds. The bottom is blue mud with three fathoms of water,
immediately outside the bar, which gradually
deepens as you recede from the shore. This bar
is about four hundred yards from the beach.
The substratum beneath the sand of the bar is
blue clay, as is also that between the bar and the
beach. This clay would afford a solid foundation for piling, by which the channel of the river
might be contracted over the bar, and thus a deep
and safe passage formed into the largest and most
important river of Texas.

The next entrance west of the Brazos, is the
Passo Cavallo, which is the inlet into the spa-
cious and beautiful bay of Matagorda. This
pass has twelve feet water over the bar, and a
safe anchorage within, with four fathoms of water. Like Galveston bay, however, this bay is
shallow. The average depth of water through
it to the mouth of the Colorado river, is not
more than eight feet. Vessels that can cross the
bay, cannot approach nearer than one mile of the
mouth of the river, and are compelled to unlade

their cargoes by means of lighters. The same inconvenience exists at the mouth of the La Baca, three feet, or three feet and a half, being the depth of water at the entrance of those rivers, at ordinary high tides.

The Colorado river is obstructed by a raft of drift wood, ten miles above the town of Matagorda. The raft fills the bed of the river and causes a dispersion of the water into several channels. The raft is not extensive, and might be easily removed. When this is accomplished the river will be navigable almost to the mountains.

Between the Brazos and the Passo Cavallo, the San Barnard river and Caney creek discharge into the gulf, but the water on their bars is very shallow.

Pursuing our course in a south-west direction, we come next to the entrance into the bay of Aransaso. This entrance is easy for vessels drawing not more than seven feet. The bay is safe and much deeper than either Galveston or Matagorda. This bay is the principal harbour for vessels whose cargoes are destined for Goliad or Bexar, and for the Irish colonies of the Neuces.

The entrance into Neuces bay is in every respect equal to that into Aransaso bay, but it has not often been resorted to. Settlements are now beginning to be formed on its margin, and all affirm that no situation for building can be more beautiful and picturesque. The margin is bold and elevated, and when the wilderness shall have given place to a respectable body of Irish emigrants, this spot will present one of the most pleasant and desirable residences in Texas.

I am perfectly satisfied that Texas is, in many respects, the most eligible part of North America. I speak of course of its natural advantages. Its civil and political condition is of course altogether prospective and uncertain. If it should hereafter become the victim of foreign domination, or the theatre of domestic oppression, it would not be the first instance of an Eden converted into an abode of sorrow and wretchedness by the folly of man. Its position is favourable for commerce. Its climate is salubrious, pleasant, and diversified, partaking of the tropical and the temperate, according to local situation. It presents every species of soil that can be found in alluvion, level, undulating, or mountainous lands, embracing all the varieties of clayey, sandy, pebbly, rocky, with all their intermixtures. It is sufficiently supplied with good timber and woodland, also with the most useful metals and fossils. Its harbours and rivers are well adapted to facilitate all the purposes of commercial intercourse both at home and abroad. Situated on the Gulf of Mexico, it has easy access to the Mexican ports on the south, to the West Indies on the east, and the United States on the north. An immense inland trade may be also carried on through the ports of Texas, with New Mexico, Chihuahua, and all the northern portion of the Mexican republic. This inland trade now passes in large caravans, from St. Louis, in Missouri, to Santa Fe, in New Mexico, through a wilderness infested with Indians. Whereas the distance from either of the ports of Texas to the Passo del Norte and Chihuahua, or New Mexico, is much less than from St. Louis, and a good wagon road may be opened the whole distance.

Nature has been bountiful in distributing her favours in Texas. Nothing now is wanting but a liberal system of policy, on the part of the government, with regard to emigration on the one hand, and a population of industrious mechanics and farmers and intelligent planters on the other,

8

to make this country rival the most favoured
parts of the earth.

And now, I suppose, you are prepared to demand a chapter on the politics of Texas. What
is the present and likely to be the future political
position of this infant Hercules? On this topic
I must disappoint you, for feeling little interest in
politics myself, I have made few inquiries on the
subject. I should say, however, that it is not
difficult to determine what, in all likelihood, will
be the future destiny of Texas. Should the
Mexican government adopt a correct policy in
relation to this country, it will form a valuable
and efficient state of the Mexican confederation,
for under a judicious system of administration, it
would not be the interest of the inhabitants to
dissolve the present connexion, and they could
feel no motive to do so. It certainly is not their
interest to separate now, nor do I believe they,
that is the more prudent and intelligent settlers,
have the least wish to do so.

It is very possible, however, that an unwise
course of administration, on the part of the
general government, might provoke a separation.
What might be the ultimate result of such a separation, I shall not attempt to conjecture.

All the attention and vigour of the settlers appears to be now, as it ought to be, directed to their own individual private concerns. If unmolested in their lawful pursuits of industry, and protected by equal laws from the imposition of the federal officers, they will be satisfied, for I cannot conceive that they should be so blind to their own interests as wantonly to resist the laws of the republic. One thing is certain, that no greater calamity could befal them than the intrusion of party politics among them. Nothing would more inevitably retard the development of the resources of the country, check emigration, and in every way thwart the benevolent purposes of heaven, and blast the present sanguine expectations of the friends of Texas, than party jealousies and party intrigue.

The question of negro slavery in connexion with the settlement of this country, is one of great importance, and perhaps may hereafter present a difficulty. The existing constitution and laws totally prohibit this worst of evils. Should this wise policy be abandoned and Texas become, what Louisiana now is, the receptacle of the redundant and jail-delivered slaves of other countries, all its energies would be paralysed, and whatever oppressions may hereafter arise either from abroad or at home, must be endured, for the country would require a prop to lean upon, and, from necessity, would be forever dependant.

Affectionately, yours, &c.

––––––––––

LETTER VIII.

Bolivar, Texas, December, 1831.

THE Comanches are a noble race of Indians, inhabiting the country to the north and north-west of San Antonio de Bexar. They are a wandering race, do not cultivate the earth for corn, but depend altogether upon the chase for subsistence. They follow the immense herds of buffaloe which graze the vast plains of this region, often to the amount of thousands in one herd. These plains are also stocked with wild horses, which run together in droves of many hundreds. These wild horses are called, in the language of the country, *Mustangs*, and hence the figure of speech to denote any thing wild and uncultivated, as a mustang girl, applied to a rude hunter's daughter. These horses are not natives, but descended from the stock brought over by the first Spaniards. Domestic animals, and man himself, become rude, when removed from the associations of civilized life. The Comanches catch and tame these wild horses, and when unsuccessful in the chase, subsist upon them.

These Indians always move on horseback. Besides the bow and arrows, the usual arms of the Indian warrior, they are armed with a long spear, having a sword blade for the point. A war party of these mounted Indians is sufficiently formidable. They are headed by two squaws, who by their shrill voices, serve as trumpeters, and have, like them, various tones, to denote the different evolutions and movements. When they descry an object of attack, or pursuit, they dart forward in a column, like lightning, towards it. At a suitable distance from their prey, they divide into two squadrons, one half taking to the right, and the other to the left, and thus surround it.

8*

Though fierce in war, they are civil in peace, and remarkable for their sense of justice. They call the people of the United States their friends, and give them protection, while they hate the Mexicans, and murder them without mercy.

The Comanches have one head chief and many subordinate ones. They hold regular councils quarterly, and a grand council of the whole tribe once a year. At these councils all important matters are decided, and all prisoners taken for offences are tried. Their discipline is rigid. If a hunting party takes the life of a North American after making him prisoner, without bringing him before the council for trial, the offenders are punished with death. Not so with the Mexicans, who are considered as enemies and treated as such. This hatred is mutual, and fully reciprocated on the part of the Mexicans. Hence the origin of the epithet expressing odium, so general in all parts of Mexico. To denote the greatest degree of degradation, they call a person a *Comanche*.

The following adventure with a body of these Indians, was related to me by Col. Austin himself. Being illustrative of the character of the Comanches, I insert it here. It will show you also, an instance of the kind of hazard, both of life and limb, which this enterprizing man has encountered in accomplishing his noble project.

On his way to the city of Mexico, in the year 1822, with but two persons in company, arriving at San Antonio, he was told it was dangerous to proceed without an escort, for a war-party of Comanches was abroad, killing every unprotected person who came in their way, that some individuals had been murdered by them the day before, and that he, with so much baggage, being a valuable prize, could not possibly hope to escape.

Finding, however, no opportunity of obtaining an escort, and the business of the colony requiring his presence in the metropolis, he resolved, at all hazards, to proceed on his journey. They travelled the first day unmolested. On the morning of the second day, feeling somewhat indisposed, he undertook to prepare some coffee. There were no accommodations on the road, and it was necessary to carry provisions on a pack-horse, and cook by the way-side. His companions warned him, that if there were Indians near, they would be attracted by the smoke. He flattered himself, that by selecting a sheltered place, and making little smoke, it would be impossible for them to discern it. Besides, his craving for the coffee was so great, being afflicted with a bad head-ache, he insisted he must have it, at all risks. They were upon an open plain, and they could see many miles around. No living creature at the moment, but themselves, was in view.

The men in company went to seek the horses, which had been hoppled the night before and let loose to feed. This is a mode of tying the horses' legs together to keep them from running away. The Colonel retired to a little ravine to enjoy his coffee. It was boiled, and in the act of putting the refreshing beverage to his parched lips, he heard a sound like the trampling of many horses. Raising his head, with the coffee yet untasted, he beheld in the distance, fifty mounted Comanches, with their spears glittering in the morning sun, dashing towards him at full speed. As the column advanced, it divided, according to their usual practice, into two semi-circles, and in an instant, he was surrounded. Quicker than thought, he sprang to his loaded rifle, but as his hand grasped it, he felt that resistance by one against a host, was vain.

The plunder commenced. Every article of the little encampment, with the saddle-bags, which he stood upon to protect if possible, was greedily seized. His presence of mind, however, did not forsake him. He calmly meditated for a moment, on what course to pursue.

Assuming great composure, he went up to the chief, and addressing him in Spanish and the few words of Indian he knew, he declared himself to be an American, and demanded if their nation was at war with the Americans. "No," was the reply. "Do you like the Americans?" "Yes— they are our friends." "Where do you get your spear heads, your blankets," &c. naming all their foreign articles, one by one. "Get them from our friends the Americans." "Well, do you think if you were passing through their nation, as I am passing through yours, they would rob you as you have robbed me?" The chief reflected a little, and replied, "No, it would not be right." Upon which he commanded his people to restore all the things taken.

Every article of value came back, with the same despatch with which it had disappeared, except the saddle-bags. These, which contained all his money, were indispensable to the further prosecution of his journey. No one could tell any thing of the saddle-bags. Almost in despair of seeing them again, he observed in a thicket, at a little distance, a squaw, one of the trumpeters, kicking and belabouring her horse, to make him move off, while the sagacious beast would not stir a step from the troop. The Colonel instantly pursued the female robber, and, thanks to her restive mustang, secured his property, which was very adroitly hidden under the saddle blanket and herself. The whole squadron then wheeled off, and were seen no more.

One little circumstance connected with this adventure must be added. A Spanish grammar, which the Colonel carried suspended at the saddlebow, that he might study it as he rode along, (for he was not then familiar with the Spanish language,) was missing. This grammar was afterwards found among the Indians by some traders, and having the owner's name in it, a report spread abroad, that he had been killed by the Comanches. This report reached the ears of his anxious mother and sister in Missouri, and it was many months before they learned that he had survived this dreary pilgrimage.

The *Carancahuas* inhabited, formerly, the whole of the sea coast. They were reputed to be cannibals and very ferocious. Hence, probably, the Spaniards were little disposed to invade them, or to visit the country without a strong military escort. Hence also, it is less surprising, that they acquired little knowledge of the coast, and thus they supplied the place of knowledge, with tales of fictitious horrors.

The first settlers in this part of the country, under Colonel Austin, arrived in considerable force, and were well armed. The Carancahuas were sufficiently peaceable so long as the settlers remained in a body, annoying them only by begging and stealing, whatever fell in their way. But when the settlers separated to explore the country for the purpose of selecting an eligible location, four of the number, who were left with the provisions and baggage to protect them, were killed by these Indians, and their goods carried off.

Thus hostilities commenced. The colonists, at this period, were not strong enough to inflict the chastisement the Indians had provoked, being unaided by a single soldier from the government, and were compelled to submit to the insolence

they could not resent. These vexations were
endured for some years, when, at last, the number of the colonists being much increased, they
mustered a party of sixty riflemen, to punish them
for some murders they had committed. Colonel
Austin commanded this expedition in person.
The result was, the slaughter of half the tribe.
The remainder took refuge in the church of the
Mexican Mission of La Bahar. The priests
were ordered to turn them out, on pain of having
the sanctuary violated in case of refusal. But,
after much entreaty, by the priests and Alcade,
a truce was granted them, on condition, that they
should never again cross the La Baca river, the
western boundary of the colony. The Alcade
and priests became surety for their good beha-
viour. This engagement, they have faithfully
kept.

Recently, the Mexicans have commenced killing the remnant of this tribe, for some robberies
and murders committed by them. The survivors
have crossed the La Baca, to the number of forty
or fifty, to beg the protection of the colonists, offering to perform any kind of service or labour,
in return for protection and food. The people

on that frontier have, accordingly, distributed them amongst their families, as servants.

Thus, the shores and bays of this beautiful region, in which these fierce children of the woods once roamed, free as the lion of the desert, have been transferred to other hands. From being the rightful proprietors of the domain, they have become the hewers of wood and drawers of water, to their invaders.

There are remnants of several other tribes of Indians, which still exist in Texas, but of too little note to merit particular notice. They are either too few in numbers to be formidable, or so far civilized, as to provide well for themselves, without disturbing others. The Cushatees are most worthy of notice. They have their villages on the Trinity river, their houses are well constructed, and their fields well cultivated. They have good stocks of horses and cattle, use culinary utensils, and are hospitable to strangers. In autumn, when their crops are laid by, they range the country in small parties, to procure a winter's stock of venison and bear's meat, leaving their villages often without a single individual to protect them. They are few in number and quite friendly. When among the settlements,

9

they conduct themselves with great propriety, and know the difference between a wild hog and one that has a mark on his ear.

The Kickapoos and Shawnees, driven by the people of the United States to the west of the Mississippi, sometimes extend their hunting parties quite to the settlements on the Brazos. They appear to regard the American settlers in Texas, as a part of the people of the United States, and conduct themselves in a friendly and respectful manner.

Affectionately, yours, &c.

LETTER IX.

Bolivar, Texas, December, 1831.

THE first settlement of this colony by Colonel Austin and his little band of hardy pioneers, displays a spirit of noble enterprise not often surpassed. If the project of establishing such a colony in Texas did not originate with the Austins, it was the first proposal of the kind that was accepted by the Mexican authorities, and it cannot be denied, that the sagacity, the prudence, the industry and perseverance, displayed by Col. Austin in the successful execution of the undertaking, are worthy of all admiration. A short history of the origin of the colony, with some of the difficulties which embarrassed its first struggles for existence, cannot fail to be interesting.

The idea of forming a settlement of North Americans in the wilderness of Texas, it is believed, originated with Moses Austin, esq. of Missouri, and, after the conclusion of De Onis' treaty, in 1819, efforts were made by him to put matters in train for an application to the Spanish government in Old Spain. In answer to his inquiries as to the best mode of laying the subject before the Spanish government, he was advised to apply to the Spanish authorities in New Spain. A memorial was accordingly presented, and his application granted, on the 17th January, 1821, by the supreme government of the Eastern Internal Provinces of New Spain, at Monterrey. Authority was hereby granted to Mr. Austin to introduce three hundred families into Texas, on terms that were satisfactory to both parties.

At this juncture of affairs, before any location for the intended colony was fixed upon, in the midst of diligent preparations to fulfil his engagement, Mr. Moses Austin died. His health had suffered greatly by exposure to bad weather, from swimming and rafting rivers, and from want of provisions on his return to Missouri from Bexar; for at that time Texas was an entire wilderness from Bexar to the Sabine. A severe cold, occasioned by this exposure, terminated in an inflammation of the lungs, which finally put an end to his mortal life.

This gentleman was a native of Durham, in the State of Connecticut, and presents an eminent specimen of the enterprising character of the New England people. At a very early age, impelled by a thirst of knowledge, and an ambition to make a speedy fortune, he left his native state, and, at the age of twenty, was married to Miss Maria Brown, in Philadelphia. Shortly afterwards, in partnership with his brother, Stephen Austin, he purchased the lead mines, called Chessel's Mines, on New river, Wythe county, Virginia, to which he removed, and established a regular system of mining and smelting, together with the manufacture of shot, sheet-lead, &c. Miners and mechanics to prosecute this business, were introduced from England, for at that time, manufactures, of this description, were in their infancy in the United States. Owing to causes beyond his control, this enterprise failed of success. Having received flattering accounts of the lead mines in Upper Louisiana, now Missouri, he resolved to visit that distant and unknown country. Accordingly, having procured the necessary passports from the Spanish minister, he visited Upper Louisiana in 1797, and procured a grant from the Governor General, Baron de Carondelet, for one league of land, including the Mine-a-Burton, forty miles west of St. Genevieve. After closing all his affairs in the United States, he removed his family, with a number of others from Wythe county, by a new and almost untried route, down the Kenhawa river, to his new grant, in 1799, and laid a foundation for the settlement, of, what is now called, Washington county, in Missouri. The early settlers of this county will bear ample testimony to his enterprise, public spirit, and honourable character. The exercise of these generous qualities, in fact, brought on another reverse of fortune, and compelled him to turn, with unabated ardour, in the decline of

9*

life, to a new and hazardous enterprise in the
wilderness of Texas.

At his death, Mr. Moses Austin left a request,
that his son, Stephen F. Austin, should prosecute
the enterprise which he had thus commenced, of
forming a settlement in Texas.   Stephen F.
Austin, whom I shall hereafter designate as Col.
Austin, immediately entered upon the prosecution of the enterprise with vigour.   After having
first visited the capital of Texas, to make the
legal arrangements, and having personally surveyed the country, without a guide, and at much
risk, in order to select a favourable location, in
December, 1821, he arrived on the river Brazos
with the first emigrants, and the new settlement
was commenced in the midst of an entire wilderness.   Without entering into a detailed history
of all the difficulties, privations and dangers that
were encountered by the first emigrants, it is sufficient to say, that such a detail would present
examples of inflexible perseverance and fortitude
on the part of these settlers, which have been
seldom equalled in any country, or in any enterprise.

Of two cargoes of provisions, shipped from
New Orleans for their subsistence, one was lost

on the coast, the other, after having been deposited on shore, was destroyed by the Carancuhuas, and four men, left to protect it, were massacred. They were compelled by these disappointments, to obtain their seed-corn over land, and with much trouble, from Sabine or Bexar. For months, they were totally destitute of bread and salt. Sugar and coffee were luxuries, enjoyed only in remembrance or in anticipation. Their only dependence for subsistence, was upon the wild game. To range the country for buffaloe, was dangerous on account of the Indians. The mustangs, or wild horses, fortunately were abundant and fat, and, it is estimated, that one hundred of them were eaten in the course of the two first years.

The Carancuhua Indians were very hostile on the coast. The Wacos and Tawakanies were equally so in the interior, and committed constant depredations. Parties of Tankaways, Lepans, and other tribes, were intermingled with the settlers. These Indians were beggarly and insolent, and were restrained from violence the first two years, only by presents, forbearance, and policy. There was not force enough in the colony to awe them. One imprudent step with these Indians, would have destroyed the settlement, and the settlers deserve as much credit for their forbearance, during the years 1822-23, as for their fortitude. In 1824, the force of the colony justified a change of policy, and a party of Tarankaways was, in that year, publicly tied and whipped, in presence of their chiefs, for horse stealing.

The hardships of the wilderness, however, were not the only difficulties to be surmounted. Great embarrassment arose from another quarter, which produced much delay, expense, personal risk, and discouragement to Col. Austin, and not only checked all further accession to the colony for a time, but compelled some of the actual emigrants to abandon their lands.

In March, Col. Austin proceeded to Bexar to make his report to the Governor, by whom he was informed, for the first time, that it would be necessary for him to proceed, immediately, to the city of Mexico, in order to procure from the Mexican Congress, then in session, a confirmation of the original grant to his father, Moses Austin, and receive special instructions as to the distribution of land, the issuing of titles, &c. This intimation was totally unexpected, and, as may be well supposed, very embarrassing; for not calculating upon any thing of the kind, he had not made the necessary preparations for such a journey. There was no time for hesitation. Hasty arrangements were made with Mr. Josiah H. Bell, to take charge of the infant settlement, and Col. Austin immediately departed for the city of Mexico, a journey of twelve hundred miles.

This was an undertaking of no little hazard at that time. Owing to the revolutionary state of the country, the roads were infested with robbers, and the Indians, taking advantage of the times, committed many outrages. Col. Austin fortunately escaped without molestation, except that of being partially robbed by a party of Comanches, as related in a preceding letter. From Monterrey, he had but one companion. They both disguised themselves in ragged clothes, with blankets, so as to pass for very poor men, who were going to Mexico to petition for compensation for services in the revolution.

The state of political affairs in the capital, at this time, was very unsettled. In addition to embarrassments likely to arise from this source, when Col. Austin arrived in Mexico, he laboured under the disadvantages of being a foreigner, a total stranger, and ignorant of the language of the country, except what little knowledge he had acquired in his first trip to Bexar, and on his journey to the capital. Without entering into a minute detail of all the perplexities and difficulties which embarrassed the business, arising out of the revolutions and frequent modifications of the general government, which took place at that period, and these were neither few nor small, Col. Austin, after a whole year's detention, at last had the satisfaction of returning to Texas, with the object of his journey fully accomplished. His authority to plant a colony in Texas, under which he had been acting, was confirmed by all the national authorities which, under different names, had ruled the Mexican nation during the year; and, as the last confirmation was by the Sovereign Constituent Congress, whose members were the acknowledged and legal representatives of the people of the nation, there could be no shadow of doubt as to the legality and validity of his concession.

In August, when Col. Austin arrived in the colony, it was nearly broken up, in consequence of his long detention in Mexico, and emigration had totally ceased. Many of the first emigrants had returned to the United States, and a number of those who had commenced their journey for the colony, had stopped in the vicinity of Nacogdoches, or on the Trinity river, and thus the settlement of those sections of country began. By energetic exertion and prudent management, however, the life of the expiring colony was soon revived, and from the day of Col. Austin's personal re-appearance in the settlement to the present day, the affairs of the colony have flowed onward, with a silent, but rapid and uninterrupted prosperity. It now numbers upwards of six thousand inhabitants, and the influx of emigrants greater than ever. These people I am assured are, as a body, of the most industrious and worthy character; for the greatest precaution has been used, from the commencement of the enterprise, to exclude the idle and the vicious. This judicious policy has been pursued throughout, from a conviction, that the success of the undertaking must depend upon the good character of the population. A report, counter to this statement, has more than once found its way to the public ear, and been circulated in the newspapers, but it is a fabrication and a slander.

Several fugitives, who found their way into the colony in 1823-4, he expelled, under the severest threats of corporal punishment if they returned, and in one instance he inflicted it. As regards the general morality and hospitality of the inhabitants, and the commission of crimes, the settlement, it is contended, will bear a favourable comparison with any county in the United States.

When, in the progress of years, the state of Texas shall take her place among the powerful empires of the American continent, her citizens will doubtless regard Col. Austin as their patriarch, and children will be taught to hold his name in reverence; for though there have been many other respectable men engaged in the work of colonization, yet Col. Austin began the work, and was the first to open the wilderness. All the subsequent labour of others has been comparatively easy.

Col. Austin has proved himself, both in point of talents and sound judgment, perfectly qualified for the arduous undertaking he took in hand. In the first place, we view him as the hardy and bold pioneer, braving all the dangers of a wilderness infested with hostile Indians, far out of the

reach of civilized society, and all the most common comforts of civilized life, enduring with the
humblest labourer of the little band, all the exposure and privation of the camp, living for months
upon wild horse-flesh, without bread or salt.

In the second place, we view him as the skilful negotiator in the capital of Mexico. His
difficulties here, were of the most trying and discouraging kind, and required the greatest discre-
tion to surmount; for his business was with the
government, and that government in a constant
state of revolution and counter-revolution. Twice
was his business brought, as he had every reason
to think, almost to a successful termination,
when a change of government threw it out, and
left him where he began months before, to com-
mence anew. His difficulties were not a little
increased by the number of petitions for grants
of colonization similar to his own. Among these
applications, was one from Gen. Wilkinson, formerly of the United States army. It argues not
a little in favour of his own skilful management,
that, of all these petitions, his alone was finally
acceded to, at that time, by the Mexican authorities.

10

Next, view him as the civil governor and military commander of the people; for he was clothed with very extensive civil and judicial authority in all matters, and, as commander of the militia, he was vested with the rank of Lieut. Colonel, by the provincial deputation of Coahuila and Texas. If his power has been great, most judiciously and beneficently has he wielded it, as is abundantly proved and illustrated, by the present prosperity of the colony. If any one is inclined to surmise, that this prosperity was a matter of course, he should reflect, that, out of twenty grants of colonization similar to his own, his, alone, can be said to have fully succeeded. Whoever will reflect upon the proverbial jealousy of the Mexican people, which, for years, was indulged to such a degree as to exclude every foreign footstep from the soil of Texas, will know how to appreciate the prudent and sagacious management which has produced such pleasing results. Nor should it be forgotten, that, whatever has been accomplished, has been effected by policy and private resources alone, without the aid of a single soldier to repel hostile Indians, or a single dollar from the public trea-

sury, even to pay the salaries of the necessary
subordinate officers and clerks.

It may be supposed, that he is now sufficiently
compensated for all his labours by a vast accumulation of wealth. But this is not so. He indeed, holds the title to much valuable land. Aside
from this, he is poor, and land can hardly be considered wealth, where land is so abundant, and
to be got almost for nothing. Many of the settlers, without any of the hardships, or exposure,
or labour, which he has encountered, are richer
than he. That many opportunities of promoting
his private fortune have presented themselves,
will, of course, be understood. But his character
is noble and generous, and he has, in a great
measure, yielded all considerations of a private
nature, to the general welfare of the colony. He
has had his enemies and calumniators, as it is natural to expect of one, who held the power, and
was determined to exercise a wholesome authority, in the management of affairs. His repu-
tation, however, remains untarnished, and never
in higher estimation than at this present moment.
Amidst all the slanderous imputations that have
been uttered against him, he finds sufficient con-
solation, in the general confidence of all the intel-

ligent and worthy part of the settlers, and above
all, in the uniform approbation of the Mexican
authorities.

The colony has received the most cordial and
uninterrupted manifestations of liberality, confidence, and kindness, from every superior officer,
who has governed the province of Texas, or the
state of Coahuila and Texas, from its commencement to the present time. For its services on
one occasion, it received, in flattering terms, the
approbation of the President. These testimo-
nials are too high and unimpeachable to leave any
doubt, as to the morality, honour, and integrity,
of either Col. Austin himself, or of the great
mass of the settlers. To say that there are no
base men here, would be a violation of candour
and truth, but these individuals meet their reward
in Texas, as in other well regulated communities, in the frowns of public opinion.

Col. Austin is still a young man, not yet forty
years of age, but, through the hardships of his
life, looks much older than he really is. In his
youth, he received a respectable academical education at Colchester, in Connecticut, but began,
very early, to acquire that species of knowledge
which is to be obtained only by the experience

of business, and the intercourse of men,—a kind
of knowledge which has qualified him to perform
well his part in the peculiar sphere of life in
which he has been called, by Providence, to act.
He is, now, a member of the Legislature of Coahuila and Texas, which holds its sittings at Sal-
tillo. Long may he live to reap the reward of
his arduous labours, and enjoy the fruits of his
noble enterprise.

We do injustice to the subject, and to the
Austins, by regarding them merely as the founders
of the colony which bears their name. They
have, in fact, been the movers, either directly or
indirectly, of the whole North American and
Irish emigration to this country, and, whatever
good may result to the great cause of liberty, of
science, and human happiness, by the introduc-
tion into this vast region, of the English language, and of those principles of republican and
constitutional government, which always accompany that language, may be very properly attributed to them,—to the father for conceiving the
idea of such an enterprise, to the son for successfully accomplishing it. Few instances occur
in the history of new settlements, in which results so important and permanent have been pro-
10*

duced by means so comparatively feeble, and
under circumstances so discouraging. The settlers of Austin's Colony were unaided by capital
or support, either from the Mexican government
or from any other quarter. They had no resources, whatever, to depend upon, except those
afforded by the spirit and prudence of their
leader, a total contempt of danger, obstacles,
and privations, and a firm reliance on their rifles,
themselves, and their God. Besides the natural
difficulties of subduing the wilderness, they had
to contend with the deeply fixed prejudices of
the people in the United States, who were loath
to remove to a country, which they had been
taught to believe, was barren and savage, doomed
to eternal pestilence and fevers, and, at least, but
a refuge for fugitive criminals, pirates, and des-
perados. Other obstacles, not less appalling to
some, arose from the revolutionary and distracted
condition of the civil government of Mexico.

Until recently, neither the Mexican government nor the Mexican people, knew any thing of
this interesting country, and, whatever value it
now possesses in their estimation, or in the opinion of the world, is to be attributed, entirely, to
the foreign emigrants. They redeemed it from

the wilderness,—they developed its resources,—
they have explored it, in its length and breadth,
and made known its geography. All has been
done by them, without the cost of a single cent
to the Mexicans. This consideration, certainly
gives to those emigrants, a natural and a just claim
upon the liberality of their government, and au-
thorises them to expect a system of colonization,
of revenue and municipal law, adapted to their
local situation and their infant state.

Affectionately, yours, &c.

LETTER X.

Bolivar, Texas, December, 1831.

THE people of Texas, as yet, have little time for
trade. Every body is occupied with his domestic arrangements and plans for supplying his immediate wants. It is found to be easier to raise
or manufacture such articles as are needed in the
family, or to do without, than to obtain them from
abroad, or to employ an individual to scour the

country, in search of such as may be desired.
People live too far apart, to beg or borrow often,
and few trouble themselves to send any thing to
market, though they have ever so much to spare.
They had rather give to you of their abundance,
if you will send to their doors. The towns are
too distant to obtain supplies from them ; while
some are too proud, some too lazy, and most too
indifferent, to trouble themselves about the matter.
If they want any article of first necessity, coffee,
for instance, which is much used, they will send
some of their chickens, butter, and eggs, to a
neighbouring family newly arrived, and propose
an exchange, as most new comers bring with
them some stores. There is much of this kind
of barter, provisions being so much more plenty
than money. Nobody, however, fares very sump-
tuously; the new comers have not the articles,
and the older residents have grown indifferent to
the use of them. Besides, they are rich enough;
without depending upon the sale of small matters
for an income.

There is a peculiar feeling among them about
game. No one will receive money for any thing
taken by his gun, but will cheerfully give you as
much as you will take, and feel insulted, if you

offer him money in return. As the chief supplies
are of this description, there is, of course, little
for sale. It would be better for the public, if this
feeling did not prevail, as provisions of this sort,
could be furnished at so easy and cheap a rate.

Hence, there is some ground for reasonable
complaint against the living in Texas. But it is
not the fault of the country. It is an evil, which
persons suitably disposed, who would open farms,
gardens, and poultry yards, in the vicinity of the
settlements, could very soon remedy, while they
would not, themselves, be the persons least bene-
fitted. In no country, with the usual attention to
the arts of life, could more luxuries for the table
be furnished. At present, vegetables, fruits, eggs,
butter, and chickens, sell very high in Brazoria;
though they are yielded in every season of the
year, in a profusion unexampled in any part of
the world. The new comer has but to plant his
seeds in the ground, and collect a first supply of
live stock to begin with. They need but little or
no care afterwards, and the increase is astonishing.
He brands his cattle and hogs, and lets them run.
They require no attention, but to see that they do
not stray too far from home, and become wild.
A field once planted in pumpkins, seldom needs

planting again. The scattered seed sow themselves, and the plants are cultivated with the corn. These pumpkins, as large, often, as a man can lift, have a sweet flavour, and are very palatable. A field of them is a curiosity, they are in such numbers and so large. Sweet potatoes, also, are cultivated with almost equal ease, and yield, at times, five hundred bushels to the acre. Some of these potatoes weigh from four, to seven pounds. Yet they sell, at Brazoria, at the enormous price of seventy-five cents a bushel. Corn is obtained in the prairie cane-brakes, the first year, when there is no time to prepare the land, with the plough, by merely making a hole for the seed, with a hoe. Cows and horses get their own living. The trees at this moment, (17th December,) are loaded with rich clusters of grapes; not very large, but of a delicious flavour.

Amidst this profusion of the good things of life, can it be difficult, with proper arrangement, to live, and to live well, in Texas? Unfortunately, cooks do not grow on trees. The epicure, therefore, who brings with him his morbid appetites, must also bring his cook.

During my stay at Bolivar, we might have had, every day, the finest of game; could any one have been spared to take the field, with his gun. Our neighbour at one hunt, brought in three bears, a Mexican hog, a rabbit and two bee-trees. Our carpenter, without leaving his bench five minutes, killed several wild ducks, the finest I ever tasted.

Affectionately, yours, &c.

LETTER XI.

Bolivar, Texas, December, 1831.

THE extensive flat country, which stretches from the coast of Texas many hundred miles, to the interior mountains, produces periodical winds, like the monsoons of India. From March to November, but little rain falls, and the power of the sun upon the flat surface of the land is such, as to exhale that little, promptly. The face of the flat region is, therefore, dry in summer, and the continual action of the sun upon a surface so extensive, flat, and dry, causes a constant indraught of air from the sea. A strong south-east wind is thus produced, which blows, almost without intermission, except at the full and change of the moon.   There are occasional interruptions, by the calms of midsummer, and by northers of slight force, and of short duration, in the spring and fall.

In November, the strong northers set in.   The rains, which usually fall in this month, cool the land.   The mountains of the interior, now covered with snow, serve as generators of cold air; while the continued action of the sun upon the waters of the gulf, rarefies the air in that direction, and consequently a strong current is produced, of the cold and heavier atmosphere of the north.   Hence, in the months of December and January, the cold northern winds sweep down the plains, with nearly as much regularity, as the south-east wind in summer; being, occasionally, interrupted by that wind, chiefly on the full and change of the moon.   In these months, the southerly winds are of short duration, and soon produce rain, an infallible indication of an immediate norther.   These northers, or northerly winds, blow sometimes from the north-west, and sometimes from the north east. The north-west is most prevalent in midwinter: the north-east, early and late in the season.   They come on very suddenly ; often without warning, always blow strong, and at times, very violently.

The effect of these winds upon the tide-water of the bays along the coast, is very perceptible. In Galveston bay a strong norther, reduces the depth of water three or four feet, and keeps out the tide until it moderates. A south-east gale has a reverse effect. On Red Fish bar, which crosses that bay, during a strong norther, there are, at times, but three and a half feet of water at high tide, but with a strong south-east wind, there are usually six feet, and sometimes seven. This observation will apply to all the bays of the coast.

These periodical winds, doubtless tend, greatly, to purify the atmosphere, and contribute much to give to the climate of Texas a blandness, which I do not recollect to have experienced any where else, and a salubrity, which we look for, in vain, in the low country of the southern United States. The climate may be described to be, in general terms, a perpetual summer. But it must not be supposed, that there are no cold days in Texas, nor exceptions here, as elsewhere, to the general course of things. The last winter, (1830,) was so severe in Louisiana, as well as in Texas, that all the young orange trees were killed, and the

11

old ones injured. Even much of the cane was destroyed. But this is a very rare occurrence. In 1831, of which I have personal experience, the northers, as they are technically called, were frequent from the middle of November until Christmas. They seldom lasted long, not more than a day or two, and were invariably succeeded by warm rains, or bright sunshine. The greatest cold produced but white frost, considered at the north, as the harbinger of mild weather, except once, when there was hail and sleet, and the ground had a slight covering of snow, the only instance except one, Col. Austin informed me, since his residence in the country. The foliage did not leave the trees, nor even the rose bushes, and the grass was verdant. Yet with summer feelings and summer dresses, and apartments not very tight, these winds were sufficiently uncomfortable. I regret not having a better thermometer than my own feelings, to give you the precise degree of cold. These cold days, however, while they last, make so small a proportion of the year, as to be hardly remembered when they are past.

Emigrants arriving during the time of which I speak, would of course, be disappointed in their

visions of the climate. It is not at all surprising,
that some, who have arrived in Texas at this un-
propitious moment, have become disheartened,
and sighed for home, or what is much less excu-
sable, have given vent to their morbid feelings,
by detraction, and slanderous misrepresentations
of the country. An old settler from Maine told
me, he had known winters here so mild, as not to
kill the Lima bean. The best month to arrive in,
is October. The first impression at that time is
delightful, as well as just, and there is less inconvenience and trouble at that time, than at any
other season. It is also the most favourable season
on account of health. The change to the hot
months of the succeeding year, is then gradual.
Those persons who come from the northern states
or from Europe, in the spring and summer, experience too sudden a change, and are always more
or less, affected by it.

House-keepers should bring with them all indispensable articles for household use, together
with as much common clothing (other clothing is
not wanted) for themselves and their children, as
they, conveniently, can. Ladies in particular,
should remember, that in a new country, they
cannot get things made at any moment, as in an

old one, and that they will be sufficiently busy, the first two years, in arranging such things as they have, without occupying themselves in obtaining more. It should also be done as a matter of economy. Where the population increases, beyond the increase of supplies, articles of necessity, as well as of luxury, are dear. If, on arrival, they find a surplus on hand, it can be readily disposed of to advantage; for trade, by barter, is much practiced, and you buy provisions, with coffee, calico, tea-kettles, and saucepans, instead of cash.

Those who *must* have a feather-bed, had better bring it, for it would take too long to make one; and though the air swarms with live geese, a feather-bed could not be got for love or money. Every body should bring pillows and bed linen. Mattresses, such as are used, universally, in Louisiana, and they are very comfortable, are made of the moss, which hangs on almost every tree. They cost nothing but the case and the trouble of preparing the moss. The case should be brought. Domestic checks are best, being cheap and light, and sufficiently strong. The moss is prepared, by burying it in the earth, until it is partially rotted. It is then washed very clean, dried and picked; when it is fit for use. These mattresses should be made very thick: and those who like a warmer bed in winter, can put some layers of wool, well carded, upon the moss, taking care to *keep this side up.*

Every emigrant should bring musqueto bars. Since the middle of October, I have not found them necessary. They are indispensable in the summer season, and are made of a thin species of muslin, manufactured for the purpose. Furniture, such as chairs and bureaus, can be brought in separate pieces and put together, cheaper and better, after arrival, than they can be purchased here, if purchased at all. But it must be recollected, that very few articles of this sort, are required, where houses are small, and building expensive. Think of the Vicar of Wakefield's picture. Tables are made by the house carpenter, which answer the purpose very well, where nobody has better, and the chief concern is, to get something to put upon them. The maxim here, is, nothing for show, but all for use. A few well selected standard books, must not be forgotten.

Hitherto, no duties have been required by the government, upon any articles, brought from any country by emigrants. The time of limitation,

11*

however, has now expired, and custom-houses
have lately been established. The rate of duty
can be ascertained, by applying to a Mexican con-
sul, from whom it is necessary to obtain passports.
No foreigner is admitted into the country, without a passport. Careful attention must be given
to these particulars, to prevent detention, and an
examination, by no means agreeable, on arrival.
It should be stated in the passport, whether the
person be really an emigrant or a trader, as the
former is allowed some privileges over the latter.

The rate of exchange, operates very favour-
ably to emigrants. At the present moment, they
may receive seven per cent., on all the money
they bring. Money is scarce, in Texas; but all
that money can purchase, and much that it can
never buy, is plenty. The poor man of industry,
should know, that he can get along without it; or
at least, with very little. Those who are so fortunate as to have it, loan it, at a very high interest, on real estate security. Fifteen and twenty
per cent. is the common rate of interest.

Affectionately, yours, &c.

LETTER XII.

Bolivar, Texas, December, 1831

ONES feelings in Texas are unique and original, and very like a dream or youthful vision realized. Here, as in Eden, man feels alone with the God of nature, and seems, in a peculiar manner, to enjoy the rich bounties of heaven, in common with all created things. The animals, which do not fly from him ; the profound stillness ; the genial sun and soft air,—all are impressive, and are calculated, both to delight the imagination, and to fill the heart, with religious emotions.

With regard to the state of society here, as is natural to expect, there are many incongruities. It will take some time for people gathered from the north, and from the south, from the east, and from the west, to assimilate, and adapt themselves to new situations. The people are universally kind and hospitable, which are redeeming qualities. Every body's house is open, and table spread, to accommodate the traveller. There are

no poor people here, and none rich; that is, none
who have much money.   The poor and the rich,
to use the correlatives, where distinction, there is
none, get the same quantity of land on arrival,
and if they do not continue equal, it is for want
of good management on the one part, or superior
industry and sagacity on the other.   All are happy, because busy; and none meddle with the affairs of their neighbours, because they have enough
to do to take care of their own.   They are bound
together, by a common interest, by sameness of
purpose, and hopes.   As far as I could learn, they
have no envyings, no jealousies, no bickerings,
through politics or fanaticism.   There is neither
masonry, anti-masonry, nullification nor court in-
trigues.

The common concerns of life are sufficiently
exciting to keep the spirits buoyant, and prevent
every thing like ennui.   Artificial wants are entirely forgotten, in the view of real ones, and self,
eternal self, does not alone, fill up the round of
life.   Delicate ladies find they can be useful, and
need not be vain.   Even privations become plea-
sures: people grow ingenious in overcoming difficulties.   Many latent faculties are developed.
They discover in themselves, powers, they did

not suspect themselves of possessing. Equally surprised and delighted at the discovery, they apply to their labours with all that energy and spirit, which new hope and conscious strength, inspire.

You wish to know my opinion, if it will do for all sorts of people to emigrate to Texas, and if I would advise J—— and S—— to sell out and remove. On this point, I should say, industrious farmers will certainly do well, and cannot fail of success; that is to say, if abundant crops, and a ready market with high prices, will satisfy them. Substantial planters, with capital and hands, may enlarge their operations here to any extent, and with enormous profits. One gentleman, for instance, whom I visited, has ninety-three acres under cultivation, by seven hands. His crop, this year, consists of eighty bales of cotton, two thousand bushels of corn, five hundred bushels of sweet potatoes, besides other articles of minor importance.

Those persons, however, who are established in comfort and competency, with an ordinary portion of domestic happiness; who have never been far from home, and are excessively attached to personal ease ; who shrink from hardship and

danger, and those who, being accustomed to a
regular routine of prescribed employment in a
city, know not how to act on emergencies, or
adapt themselves to all sorts of circumstances,
had better stay where they are. There is no better advice, than, " to let well enough alone." All
changes may be for the worse as well as better,
and what we are used to, though not so good as
might be, may suit us best. New shoes, though
handsomer and better than old ones, may pinch
and fret the wearer. Happiness is relative. A
high standard for one person, is a low one for
another, and what one prizes, another may think
worthless. So that even conceding all the advantages I have claimed for Texas, it does not follow
that the happiness of all would be promoted, by
emigrating to this country. It depends much
upon the spirit of the man.

He whose hopes of rising to independence in
life, by honourable exertion, have been blasted by
disappointment; whose ambition has been thwarted
by untoward circumstances; whose spirit, though
depressed, is not discouraged; who longs only for
some ample field on which to lay out his strength;
who does not hanker after society, nor sigh for
the vanished illusions of life; who has a fund of

resources within himself, and a heart to trust in God and his own exertions; who is not peculiarly sensitive to petty inconveniences, but can bear privations and make sacrifices, of personal comfort—such a person will do well to settle accounts at home, and begin life anew in Texas. He will find, here, abundant exercise for all his faculties, both of body and mind, a new stimulus to his exertions, and a new current for his affections. He may be obliged to labour hard, but riches are a very certain reward of his exertions. He may be generous, without fear of ruin. He will learn to find society in nature, and repose in solitude, health in exertion, and happiness in occupation. If he have a just ambition, he will glow with generous pride, while he is marking out an untrodden path, acting in an unhackneyed sphere, and founding for himself, and his children after him, a permanent and noble independence.

Affectionately, yours, &c.

APPENDIX.

QUESTIONS RELATIVE TO TEXAS,

BY THE

LONDON GEOGRAPHICAL SOCIETY.

Note.—The following answers, it will be remarked, have, in some respects, exclusive reference to Austin's Colony, though, with few exceptions, they are equally applicable to the whole country. It is to be hoped, that the omission, either in these answers or in the preceding letters, of more extended notices of other colonies in Texas, will not be regarded as any disparagement of those colonies. The author's visit was to Austin's Colony alone, where opportunities of inquiry respecting the local concerns of the other colonies, did not occur. Whatever notices of these colonies she might have been disposed to insert in this volume, must necessarily, have been compiled from the printed documents of the companies engaged in colonization, already before the public. To these documents, she must refer the reader for any local information that may be desired. It may be stated here, that efforts were made by the editor, to procure, from the persons concerned, a general statement of the condition of all the colonies and grants, that have been authorized by law, in Texas, that the public might have the whole subject presented in one view. The work was, actually delayed more than a month, waiting for a statement of this sort, which was promised by a gentleman every way qualified to prepare it. A pressure of important business, alone, prevented him from accomplishing his intention.

QUESTION FIRST.—*The proportion of land taken up by the Americans and on what title? Which of the susceptibilities of the soil are they inclined to develope?*

The largest portion of land taken up by foreign emigrants, is in Austin's Colony, which contains, (1831,) six thousand inhabitants, principally Americans, though there are a

12

number of Irish and English, and some Germans and French.
The colonization law of the State of Coahuila and Texas,
grants one league of land to families, and a quarter of a
league to single men.   A Mexican league, is 5000 Mexican
varas square ; equal to 4428 acres English measure.   The
vara is 8 per cent. less than the English yard.   The quantity
of land distributed in Austin's Colony, with legal titles, is,
about 1400 leagues.

   In the colony contracted by De Witt, on the Gaudalupe
river, upwards of two hundred leagues have been granted
to American emigrants, settled by him, and about an equal
number of leagues, to native Mexicans.   The Irish colonies
contracted for by Messrs. MacMullen and McGlone, on
the Nueces, and that of Messrs. Powers and Hewitson, on
the coast, between the La Baca and Nueces rivers, are in
a progressive state, but it is not known, how many leagues
have been distributed, under these contracts.   The country
on the San Antonio river, with that on the lower portion of
the Gaudalupe, is granted principally, to Mexicans, who
reside in Bexar and Goliad.   The extensive country lying
east of Austin's Colony as far as the Sabine river, is holden
under contracts of colonization, by several respectable companies and individuals, who are successfully engaged in appropriating their lands, but the number of leagues distributed by them, cannot be stated.

   Titles.—Col. Austin, has entered into five contracts, of
different dates, with the Mexican government, to colonize
a number of families, not exceeding two thousand.   Of
these obligations, two have been already completed.   One
will expire in 1833, and another in 1834.   The last of the
above-mentioned contracts, was made in February, 1831,
and, like all the others, will be in force for six years from
the date of it.

   The emigrant, after being duly admitted by Austin as
a colonist, under his contract, receives a title from the
commissioner of the government, for the quantity of land
assigned him, by law.   This commissioner is appointed by
the governor of the state, and the title issues in the name
of the state, on stamp paper, which costs from two to three
dollars.   The whole cost of a league of land, to the settler,
will, generally, be about four cents an acre.   For a part of
the sum a credit is given, of four, five and six years.   All
land titles in Texas are granted in this manner, whether to
foreigners or Mexicans, and are all subject to the condition

of being forfeited to the state, if the grantee fail to make
actual settlement, and to cultivate his land, within six years,
from the date of his deed, or neglect to pay the sums of
money required by law. All right and title to the land are
also forfeited, if the grantee abandon the country, or sell
his land, before having cultivated it. Mexicans, however,
who obtain lands from the government by purchase, and not
as mere settlers, have the privilege of selling it, before
actual settlement or cultivation, but the second purchaser,
is bound to do both, within six years from the date of the
original title, or forfeit the land.

The settlements in Austin's Colony, extend quite down
to the gulf shore, and to the margins of Galveston and
Matagorda bays. None are settled in this colony without
legal titles, and, consequently, there are no *Squatters* here.

Articles principally cultivated.—The principal occupation
of the foreign emigrants is, farming and raising black cattle,
horses, mules, &c. Cotton, sugar, maize or Indian corn,
beans, sweet potatoes and vegetables of all sorts, are successfully cultivated. The cotton produced here, is of very
superior quality, and yields from 2500 to 3000 pounds of
seed-cotton, to the acre. Seventy-five bushels of Indian
corn to the acre, have been, frequently gathered: but it is
not usual for the farmers to bestow a sufficiency of labour
on their corn crops, to produce that quantity, generally.

QUESTION SECOND.—*What are the natural productions ?*

The natural productions of Texas, are, in general, the
same with those of Louisiana and Florida. The indigenous
indigo of Texas, is considered, by those who have tried it,
to be greatly superior to the plant which is cultivated in
the United States. It is manufactured in families, for domestic use, and is preferred to the imported indigo.

The productions which may be considered as naturally
adapted to the soil of Texas, and which may be made profitable by cultivation, are short and long staple cotton,
sugar, indigo, tobacco, olives, grapes, rice, wheat, Indian
corn, rye, oats, barley, flax, hemp, sweet and Irish potatoes.
The extensive natural pastures found in the prairies, furnish
peculiar facilities for rearing horses, black cattle, hogs,
sheep and goats. Butter and cheese may be made in very
great quantities, and of superior quality. The honey-bee
seems to have found a favourite haunt in Texas. These industrious insects swarm in great abundance in every district,
and bees-wax and honey may be produced in any quantity,

and without the least expense. White or bleached bees-wax, generally sells for one dollar a pound, in the cities of Mexico. Texas is, without doubt, equal, and perhaps superior to Cuba, for bees, and will rival that island, in the exportation of honey and wax.

Dried fruits and distilled spirits, may be estimated as important articles of produce:—of the former, peaches, figs, grapes, &c.—of the latter, whiskey, peach and grape brandy, and rum.

The mulberry is a common forest tree throughout Texas, and affords every facility that can be desired, for the rearing of silk-worms.

The country between the San Jacinto and Sabine rivers, is for the most part, heavily timbered with pine. On the Brazos and Colorado, there are great quantities of live oak and cedar; so that the lumber business cannot fail to become an object of importance, at some future day.

QUESTION THIRD.—*The water, whether good or bad,—abundant or scarce ?*

The water, generally speaking, is good, in all parts of Texas. Springs of water, do not, indeed, abound, near the coast, but here the supply of water from the numerous rivers and creeks, which intersect the country, is abundant, and of good quality. Cool and refreshing water may be obtained from wells of moderate depth, in every portion of the country. The interior and undulating districts of Texas, are sufficiently watered to supply all the demands of the farmer, grazier, and manufacturer.

QUESTION FOURTH.—*What are the materials for building ?*

Materials for building are abundant. There is a sufficiency of timber for all the purposes of building, in most districts. Excellent clay, for bricks, is found in all parts. On the coast, lime may be obtained from shells and in the interior, from lime-stone. The price of lumber, at present, is high—not, however, from a scarcity of materials, but from a scarcity of saw-mills, and the high price of labour. On which account, emigrants will find their advantage, in bringing plank, scantling, window-sash, &c. with them.

QUESTION FIFTH.—*What is the current money ?*

Specie is the only current money of the country. There are no banks here, and no such thing as paper money. The greatest part of the silver coin in circulation in Texas, is of the description called provincial, or hammered and sand dollars;—a coin of the revolution, made by the Mexican patriots, before they obtained possession of any of the mints. This coin circulates at par in the state of Coahuila and Texas, and in the other eastern states: but is received at a discount of 8 or 9 per cent. in the banks of New-Orleans, and other parts of the United States. This produces a rate of exchange, highly favourable to the emigrants; for merchants, who have remittances to make to the United States, always prefer exchanging their provincial money, at the discount, for United States' bills, gold coin, or standard silver dollars. Several emigrants have found the difference of exchange, sufficient to defray all the expenses of their passage to the country.

QUESTION SIXTH.—*The harbours discovered, their depth and the soil in their neighbourhood ?*

Galveston harbour has twelve feet of water over the bar. Within the bar, it is safe and commodious. There are no settlements in the immediate vicinity of the harbour. The nearest settlement is the town of Anahuac, or that at the mouth of the San Jacinto, each forty miles distant, in a north and north-west direction up the bay, with the exception of a single family at the west end of Red-Fish bar.

The next entrance west of Galveston, is the mouth of the Brazos river, which has six feet over the bar, and a safe anchorage within. The flourishing town of Brazoria is situated on this river, thirty miles by water, and fifteen by land, from its mouth. This entrance is much the most eligible for emigrants who are bound to Austin's Colony. It is the route most frequented, and offers the best facilities for procuring the common necessaries that are needed on arrival, as well as the means of transportation into the interior.

The Passo Cavallo, or entrance into Matagorda bay has twelve feet of water over the bar, and safe anchorage within. But the bay is shallow, and will not admit of more than seven feet draught, to the mouth of the Colorado river. At the mouth of the Colorado, there is a new town, called Matagorda, which is flourishing, and is a convenient landing place for emigrants, who are destined for the western parts of Austin's Colony.

Near the mouth of La Baca, on the east side of the river, there is a considerable settlement of Americans, which belongs to Austin's Colony, and on the west side, a

12*

settlement of Mexicans. This is the best landing place for those who are bound to the Guadalupe river, or the La Baca and Navidad. Lighters are required to unlade vessels, both at the town of Matagorda, and at the mouth of La Baca.

Aransaso bay, the port of those destined for the Irish colonies on the Neuces, is similar to the preceding.

The soil in the vicinity of all these harbours and bays, is of the first quality for cultivation, but there is a scarcity of trees suitable for timber.

QUESTION SEVENTH.—*"How far north have the Mexicans settled, and what do they pursue for a livelihood?"*

The principal settlement of Mexicans, is at the old Spanish town of Bexar and Goliad, (formerly called La Bahia.) The former is the capital of Texas and contains 2500 inhabitants. The latter is a village containing about 800 inhabitants. There is, also, a small village of Mexicans on the Guadalupe, at a place called Victoria, about twenty miles from the mouth of the La Baca, near which, there is also a military post. At Nacogdoches and in the vicinity of the town, there is a Mexican population of about 500 souls. A few Mexican families are dispersed among the American settlers, particularly in Austin's Colony. They are employed by the settlers mostly as herdsmen, and are universally acknowledged to be the best hands that can be procured, for the management of cattle, horses and other live stock. The occupation of the Mexicans in Texas, generally, is raising live stock, and agriculture on a limited scale. Many of them make a business of catching and taming *Mustangs* or wild horses, which they sell to the American settlers.

QUESTION EIGHTH.—*"Which of the agricultural implements should be provided by emigrants?"*

Emigrants should provide themselves with the principal iron agricultural implements and tools, in common use in other countries; such as ploughs, hoes, axes, brush and hay scythes, harrow teeth, chains, &c. &c. In Texas, as in other countries, there is a diversity of opinion as to the best construction of the plough. The only kind used by the Mexicans, here, and in all parts of Mexico, is, what may very properly be called, the *primitive* plough. It is formed of one stick of timber only. A tree is sought for with a long straight body. One end of this is made to answer the purpose of a tongue. Near the other end a fork projects, at an angle of 45 degrees, about one foot long, having a strap of iron fixed to the end. This is the part which breaks the ground. On the upper side and just at the extremity of the main stick is the handle, by which, when in operation, the plough is kept erect, and guided by the ploughman. This simple plough is similar to that which is called a coulter plough. It serves to loosen the earth to a considerable depth, without turning it over, and is preferred by the Mexicans for this reason. They say that experience, in the Island of Cuba and in other hot climates, has proved, that the use of such ploughs as turn over the soil at every furrow, impoverishes the land, and wears it out in a few years, by exposing it, too much, to the action of a burning sun. Many farmers use the coulter and bull-tongue ploughs.

A box of tools, containing, saws, augers, chisels, a broad axe, planes, a drawing knife, square and compasses, &c. is indispensable, as these tools are needed to make the wooden part of all farming implements, as well as for the construction of buildings. Strong cart wheels, suitable for plantation use, must be provided, as articles of this sort are not yet manufactured in Texas.

QUESTION NINTH.—*What is the best mode of emigrating from the British Islands?*

The best mode of emigrating from the British Islands, is, to embark directly, for some of the harbours of Texas, in a vessel drawing not more than six feet of water, which will admit of navigating the bays, and crossing the bars. Large ships might anchor off the mouth of the Brazos river, within five hundred yards of the shore, and discharge, by the aid of lighters: but as no vessels of this class, have ever yet touched at this place, boats suitable for lighters, have not been provided. There are always a few good yawls, at the pilot's house; but a ship ought to rely mainly upon its own boats, to unlade.

October and November, are much the most favourable months for emigrants to arrive. During these months, the winds are light, and vessels of any size, may ride at anchor, off the mouth of the Brazos and other harbours, with perfect safety, and discharge their cargoes without inconvenience or delay. In these months, no danger is to be apprehended from sickness, and provisions are more abundant, than at any other season of the year.

QUESTION TENTH.—*What seeds and fruits are most needed?*

Emigrants ought to bring every kind of seed they can procure; for though seeds and fruits, of various kinds, are to be found in Texas, they are not always to be obtained without trouble and expense. The quality of many vegetables and fruits, degenerates through careless cultivation or the effect of climate. Little attention has, hitherto, been paid to the cultivation of fruit, and the country is imperfectly supplied with the choicer varieties. The climate and soil are well adapted, to all the varieties of the peach, nectarine, apricot, plum, pear, and grape. In the interior, the apple, cherry, and smaller fruits, and near the coast, all the more hardy tropical fruits succeed very well, while, with a little care, the more delicate ones, may be brought to perfection.

Seeds of small grain and grass, are scarce, such as wheat, rye, barley, buckwheat, &c. timothy, clover, and other grasses. Thorns suitable for permanent hedges, are very desirable.

Of domestic animals, emigrants from England who can afford it, should bring the best breed of English cattle, and the *grass hog*. The prairies afford vast natural pastures for these animals. Also a few blooded horses, to intermix with the light and active Andelusian breed of Mexican horses. Merino and other fine wool sheep are needed, to improve the native stock. The expense of raising sheep and goats, is so very trifling here, that it does not enter into the list of farm expenditures. Sheep require no feeding, either in summer or winter, the natural pasture being always sufficient.

COMMUNICATION

FROM SAN FELIPE DE AUSTIN,

RELATIVE TO LATE EVENTS IN TEXAS, 1832.

Remark.—Prior to the events detailed in the following communication, the citizens of Texas had been provoked, by several illegal and tyrannical acts of the military officers of the general government. They made a manly effort to relieve themselves of their immediate oppressors, and succeeded. In the accomplishment of their patriotic resolve, they proceeded in a very determined, but most orderly manner. There was not the least insurrectionary spirit manifested by them, or any wish to oppose the laws of the country. They hailed, with joy, the success of Gen. Santa Anna's party, as the pledge of a more just and liberal administration of the general government. The following communication is deemed important, as illustrative of the political feelings of the people. While the events herein recorded, exhibit on their part, an honourable sensitiveness to oppression, and a determination to resist it, at all hazards, the tranquillity which has every where prevailed throughout the state, since they took place, satisfactorily attest the peaceable and orderly disposition of the settlers, when unmolested in their rights.

The 25th of July, of the present year, was a day of jubilee to the citizens of *San Felipe de Austin*, on account of the return of Col. S. F. Austin, representative from Texas in the Legislature of the State of Coahuila and Texas, and founder of this colony, who had been absent in the interior near five months. He left Matamoras on the 14th July, in the schr. Mexico, one of five vessels which had on board 400 men of the troops of Gen. Santa Anna, commanded by Colonel Mexia, formerly Mexican Charge d'Affaires at Washington. The fleet arrived off the mouth of the river *Brazos* on the 16th, and Colonels Mexia and Austin having landed immediately, they proceeded to Brazoria, where they arrived on the 17th, and were received in the most enthusiastic manner, as is seen by the account of the proceedings on the occasion published in the Gazette of that town.

On the afternoon of the 23d, Col. Mexia, having regulated the custom-house department, and other public matters, at Brazoria, in the most satisfactory and harmonious manner, departed to embark for Galveston and Anahuac.

Col. Austin left Brazoria on the evening of the same day, and arrived, as above mentioned, at *San Felipe*, on the 25th. There a meeting of the citizens had been held for the purpose of acting in concert, to give him such a reception as was judged suited to the occasion. They had organized from amongst themselves a volunteer company, under the title of *The Santa Anna Volunteer Company*, of which F. W. Johnson, commander of the Santa Anna forces in the late expedition against the military post of Anahuac, had been elected Captain ; F. Adams, 1st Lieut.; Thomas Gay, 2d Lieut.; and Robt. Peebles, Standard Bearer.

On the morning of the 25th, an escort, commanded by Lieut. Gay, met the Colonel at the distance of 6 miles from San Felipe. At 11 A. M. the Colonel, with the escort, made his appearance, and was received by the company, paraded for the purpose in the square, where he was addressed by W. W. Jack, Esq. in the name of the company, as follows :

"Colonel Austin,—In the name of the Santa Anna Volunteer Company, composed of your friends and fellow-citizens, I, as their humble organ, take this opportunity to greet you with the most heartfelt welcome. Your return at this period is peculiarly fortunate, for while it is a source of personal gratification, it is equally well calculated to inspire with confidence all of us who are engaged in the same great and good cause.

"We have not assembled, sir, to flatter or caress you. Such conduct would be as humiliating to us as it would be disagreeable to you. A free people will never admit that such a course should be pursued towards a faithful servant; but they are always ready to concede to merit that reward to which it is entitled.

"Such a boon then as is due to him who has faithfully discharged his duties, we grant to you, with an assurance that the man whom the people have delighted to honour, still has our most unbounded confidence. The occasion of your unexpected return to Texas, will long be remembered. The present is an epocha in the political affairs of our country, on which the pen of the historian will dwell with peculiar pleasure. It is a date from which will be computed the regeneration of our beloved country; and that Texas has contributed to the bringing about of such an event, will always be a source of laudable exultation.

"In conclusion, I cannot perhaps better express my own feelings and those of our common countrymen, than by saying—well done, good and faithful servant; thou art welcome, thrice welcome, to thy home and to thy friends; and may health and happiness always attend thee."

To this address the Colonel made the following reply:

"Fellow-citizens, and Soldiers of the Santa Anna Volunteer Company,—I have not words duly to express my grateful feelings and unfeigned thanks for the kind welcome with which you have honoured my return to this colony. In all my acts, as far as they have been connected with the advancement of Texas, I have been governed by the most sincere desire to promote its prosperity and the permanent happiness of its citizens. My leading motto has been and is, *fidelity to the constitution of our adopted country.* The same has been and is, the governing principle of the inhabitants of this colony. I thank my fellow-citizens for their approbation; it is the highest reward that can be offered to me for my humble services as their public agent.

"I accord with you in the opinion, that the present is an important epocha in the political march of our adopted and beloved country. With institutions founded on the broad basis of representative democracy, the general government of Mexico has, for the last two years, been administered, in many particulars, on principles which more properly belong to a military despotism than to a free republic. A great and glorious regeneration is taking place; the free democracy of the nation, THE PEOPLE, have asserted their rights under the banner of that distinguished patriot and leader, GEN. ANTONIO LOPEZ DE SANTA ANNA.—The cause of constitutional democratic liberty is about to triumph throughout the whole of this vast republic.

"Borne down, in this remote section of the nation, by military oppression, and by the most shameful violations of the rights of the state of Coahuila and Texas, you believed that all the guarantees of the constitution and laws were disregarded and trampled upon. Patience itself was exhausted, and you had recourse to arms, thus espousing that cause of the constitution and of the people which is so bravely advocated by Gen. Santa Anna. In doing this you have not, for one moment, lost sight of your duty as Mexican citizens, but have defended the true dignity of the national flag, which had been insulted by the violators of the constitution. In the course you have taken you will be sustained by Col. Mexia, who has come to Texas with a fleet and forces, under the orders of Gen. Santa Anna to protect the rights of the nation and of the state; and you will receive the support and approbation of Gen. Santa Anna himself, of Gen. Mortezuma, and of all liberal and enlightened Mexicans. In such a cause you have nothing to fear—IT IS JUST, and I will give my hearty co-operation, so far as my feeble services can avail."

At the conclusion of this address, the Colonel was saluted with 12 rounds of cannon and small arms; after which, attended by the civil authorities, at the head of the company, he proceeded on the road to his quarters at the edge of the town, and was met by the regular troops, lately under the command of Lieut. Col. Ugartecha, in fort Velasco, at the mouth of the Brazos, and then commanded by Lieut. Moret, who after having given a salute of two rounds of small arms which was returned by the Santa Anna Company, fell into the line, and the whole marched to the Col's. quarters where he addressed the regular troops in Spanish, as follows :

" I thank you, in the name of the inhabitants of this colony, for this manifestation of your friendly sentiments towards them. It is but a short time since you and they were in hostile array against each other at fort Velasco: that was a political contest merely between citizens under the same national flag, not a war between enemies. The contest, over, each party only remembered that they were all Mexicans, and forgot that a difference of political opinions had for a short time made them belligerents. As Mexicans I now embrace you, for an evidence that *we*, the people of this colony, are such also, and that we duly appreciate the motives which have led you voluntarily to join in welcoming my return."

Col Austin then embraced the Mexican officers, amidst cheers of *viva la federacion y la constitucion Mejicana.* The whole company then partook of refreshments and retired.

At 4 o'clock the citizens and the military again assembled, and partook of a plentiful dinner, provided for the occasion. Each State and Territory of the Mexican Republic was toasted separately by name, and a salute of cannon fired for each. After which, Col. Austin rose and said: "We have drank to the prosperity of each state and territory of the Mexican confederation, and I now beg to offer as a sentiment,—the shield and bond of union of them all, *the constitution*, and Gen. Santa Anna, is defender."

Lieut. Moret, of the regular troops, then gave this sentiment: "May the Supreme Being preserve the life of Col. Austin to the citizens of Texas, twenty years and longer, so that they may have the benefit of his exertions to separate Texas from Coahuila, and form it into a State of the great Mexican Confederation, as the only means of securing its prosperity, and the true interests of the Mexican republic."

The Alcalde, in the name of the Ayuntamiento, gave "Union, the Constitution, and Gen. Santa Anna, their defender."

F. W. Johnson gave "The State of Texas and the State of Coahuila: may their political separation be the bond of union between them."

Besides the toasts thus particularised, many others were given, all expressing, in one way or other, the sentiments of *union with Mexico; support of the constitution; separation from Coahuila; and encouragement of emigration.* The greatest harmony prevailed throughout the whole entertainment.

On the 27th, a general meeting of citizens, summoned by the Ayuntamiento of the jurisdiction, was held at San Felipe; and the assembly unanimously adopted an exposition and resolutions, which explained the causes and nature of the late events at Anahuac and Brazoria, and formally declared their own adhesion to the Santa Anna party. This measure, adopted as it has been, with the co-operation and advice of Col. Austin, publicly given at the meeting, has united the people of the colony fully, many of whom were doubtful as to the course to be taken in the peculiarly critical situation of public affairs, unexpectedly precipitated, as they had been, under the excitement caused by Col. Bradburn's illegal and arbitrary imprisonment of several of the citizens. Austin's Colony is therefore now identified with the Santa Anna party ; and information received from Bexar, La Bahia and Nacogdoches, justifies the opinion

13

that all Texas will unite on the same side of the great political question, which now agitates the Mexican nation.

In order to prevent any misconstructions, it is proper and necessary to state, that the people of Austin's Colony will most decidedly oppose any attempt to separate Texas from the Mexican confederation, and that they will as decidedly insist, by all just and constitutional means, that the embarrassments in the way of emigration to Texas, be removed, so that it may, as speedily as possible, be formed into a state of the Mexican Union, separate from Coahuila, the river *Neuces* being the dividing line. There is no doubt that all Texas will be governed by the same leading principle.

Exposition made by the Ayuntamiento and inhabitants of Austin's Colony, explanatory of the late commotions, and adhering to the plan of Santa Anna. Adopted, July 27th, 1832.

The causes of the late disturbances are plain to every person who resides in Texas, or is informed of the events which have transpired here since the commencement of the year 1830; but as those causes have never been laid before the Mexican people, it is necessary and proper that it should now be done, as a justification of the course taken by a large and respectable portion of the inhabitants, and also as explanatory of the reasons which have impelled the Ayuntamiento and the inhabitants of this colony unanimously to adhere to the plan of Vera Cruz.

From the time when a national and state law invited persons of all nations to come and settle in the wilderness of Texas, *duties* and *rights* were established between those who govern and those who were to obey in virtue of them. Those laws and the general and state constitutions have clearly designated the guarantees which secure the citizens from the caprice and the arbitrary will of the subaltern authorities. But unfortunately, since the present administration went into power, an uninterrupted series of depradations, calumnies and injustice, has been the recompense received by the citizens of Texas for their firm adhesion to the Mexican republic and to the federal system by which it is governed. The civil authorities have been viewed by the military as mere subalterns, to be commanded as a corporal commands a soldier. This military power, under the authority of the superior chief, has disregarded all the rights which the constitution secures to free citizens, and has wished to subject every thing to its enslaving influence. The government of the state of Coahuila and Texas has not exercised in these colonies any more power than what the superior military chief has been pleased to grant as a favour.

To enumerate in detail all the violations of the constitution and laws, and attacks upon the rights of the state of Coahuila and Texas, which have been committed by the military authority, would occupy more time and space than the present occasion will admit; only a few of the leading ones will therefore be mentioned, which have had a direct influence in producing the late disturbances.

First—On the 22d April, 1828, concessions of land were made in conformity with the colonization laws by the president of the nation, Don Guadalupe Victoria, and the governor of this state, to the inhabitants established east of the San Jacinto, and in the district of Nacogdoches. In the year 1830, Don Jose Francisco Madero was appointed by the governor, commissioner to survey the said land, and issue the titles in due form of law to said settlers. He arrived on the Trinity river in the month of January, 1831, and had made some progress in the discharge of his duties, when he and his surveyor, Jose Maria Carbajal, were arrested by Col. Juan Davis Bradburn, military commandant of Anahuac, and conducted to that post, as prisoners. The only reason given by said commandant for this direct and insulting attack upon the constitution and sovereignty of the state of Coahuila and Texas, was, that the arrest of Madero was made in obedience to the orders of his excellency the commandant Gen. Don Manuel de Miersy Teran. Similar orders were issued for the arrest of Madero to Col. Don Jose delas Peidras, commandant of the frontier at Nacogdoches. His excellency the Governor of the state speaks of this affair in his message to the legislature at the opening of the session on the 2d January last, in the following words, as translated :

"The public tranquillity has not been disturbed in any part of the state, although Col. Davis Bradburn assumed the power without the knowledge of this government, to arrest a commissioner appointed by it, to survey vacant lands and issue titles,—which act might have caused a commotion; but nothing of the kind occurred, owing to the prudence of the arrested person, and of the citizens who were to have received titles for lands, and who by this event were deprived for the time being from obtaining legal possession of their property. This government endeavoured to ascertain the cause of this interference, and for that purpose entered into continued communications with the commandant general of the states, and so learned, that said general thinks, that agreeably to the commission conferred upon him by the supreme government of the union, under the 3d article of the national law of 6th April, 1830, the commission of said arrested commissioner was in opposition to the 11th article of said general law; and notwithstanding he has been assured that such is not the case, he still persists in his opinion. For these reasons, this matter is in such a situation, that to remove the obstacles it would be necessary to adopt measures that *might compromit the state to the highest degree.*"

Second—On the 10th December last, the commandant general, by a laconic military order, annulled the Ayuntamiento of liberty, which was legally established by the commissioner Madero, and established a new Ayuntamiento at Anahuac, without any authority from the state government, and without even consulting it.

Third—The commandant general has without any authority from the state, taken possession of, and appropriated such lands as he deemed proper; thus totally disregarding the rights and sovereignty of the state. Speaking of this subject, the governor, in the before mentioned message, says, (as translated.) "Although this government, in the message of last year, expressed a hope, that under the provisions of the law of 6th April, 1830, a considerable colonization of the vacant lands in the department of Bexar might be expected, nothing has been done up to the present time. The commissioner of the general government, notwithstanding the instructions he has received, to purchase from the state a portion of vacant lands, has not entered into the necessary contracts for this purpose, nor made any propositions to do so; but has, without any authority, occupied many points with garrisons. This government is ignorant of the causes of this strange mode of proceeding, and therefore cannot state what they are."

Fourth—The government of the state ordered U. B. Johnston, the Alcalde of liberty, to convene the people and

hold an election for Alcalde and members of the Ayuntamiento of liberty, notwithsanding the order of Gen. Teran,
before cited, annulling that corporation. Col. Bradburn
issued orders, and repeated and reiterated them, to said
Johnston, prohibiting him from proceeding with said election, and threatening him with military force; in consequence of which, the election was not held, and thus the
order of the state government was disregarded by the military power, and the citizens were by military force prevented from exercising the rights of suffrage which the
constitution and laws guaranteed to them.

Fifth—Col. Bradburn has at various times, and without
any regard whatever to the constitution or the authorities
of the state of Coahuila and Texas, arrested peaceable and
quiet citizens, for no other reason than an expression of
opinion against his violent and arbitrary acts; and he has
disregarded the rights of persons and of property, which
were expressly guaranteed by the national and state constitutions, and attempted to make every thing bend to military despotism and martial law. Encouraged by the patience of the state government, under the iron rod of military power, his despotism reached its highest point. In the
month of May last, he imprisoned seven citizens, and attempted to arrest George M. Patrick, the first regidor, and
acting Alcalde of Anahuac, and Jas. Lindsey, another
regidor of the Ayuntamiento of that place, who, in consequence, left Anahuac, and fled to Austin's Colony for security.

These repeated and continued acts of despotism, added
to the highly abusive manner in which Col. Bradburn expressed himself against the citizens, and his threats against
the constitutional authorities of the state, finally exhausted
the patience of all, and caused an excitement which spread
through every part of the country. The quiet and peaceable
citizens had looked on in silence, with their eyes and hopes
directed to the state government, as the only constitutional
authority competent to remedy evils of such magnitude, but
unfortunately the state government was then borne down
by the same iron rod that was held over Texas. His excellency, the governor, in his message before quoted, very
plainly says that he cannot sustain the constitution and law
of the state against military encroachments, without *com-
promitting the public tranquillity in the highest degree,* which is
saying in substance, that a resistance by force was the only

13*

alternative left to him, and this he was not authorized to adopt, without the previous sanction of the legislature. His excellency, therefore, did all he could without an open declaration of war against the military.

In this state of things, the citizens, goaded to desperation by military despotism on the one hand, and seeing on the other, that the state government had in vain made every effort of a pacific nature to sustain itself, and protect them, considered that petitions made on paper, were useless, that they would in fact only have given new opportunities to the military to ridicule and trample upon the state authorities, and to rivet their chains more firmly.

The last and only remedy left to an oppressed people, was then resorted to, and without any previous combinations, or organized plans, a large number of citizens, moved by a common and simultaneous influence, took up arms, and marched to Anahuac, to release the prisoners whom Bradburn had illegally confined, to re-establish the Ayuntamiento of liberty, and to prove to him that the state of Coahuila and Texas, could not any longer be trampled upon with impunity by the military power. Such were the causes and the only ones which produced the attack upon Juan Davis Bradburn, at the military post of Anahuac.

Notwithstanding the efforts of the administration of Bustamente to conceal the situation of things, the people by this time had learned that the exercise of military despotism was not confined to Texas, but that the whole republic was governed by the same iron sceptre; that the same causes which had disturbed the public tranquillity here, had roused the spirit of the free and enlightened Mexicans in every part of this great confederation, and that on the 2d January last, the heroic city of Vera Cruz had pronounced in favour of the constitution and laws, headed by the distinguished patriot Gen. Don. Antonio Lopez de Santa Anna, and being convinced that the last hope of liberty and the principles of the representative democratic federal system, depended on the success of the liberal party, of which Santa Anna was the leader, the citizens who were under arms against Bradburn, at the camp on Turtle Bayou, near Anahuac, on the 13th June, ananimously adhered to the plan of Vera Cruz, by adopting the following resolutions:

Resolved, That we view with feelings of the deepest regret, the manner in which the government of the republic of Mexico is administered by the present dynasty; the repeated violations of the constitution; the total disregard of the law; the entire prostration of the civil authority, and the substitution in its stead of a military despotism, are grievances of such a character as to arouse the feelings of every freeman, and impel him to resistance.

Resolved, That we view with feelings of the deepest interest and solicitude, the firm and manly resistance, which is made by the highly talented and distinguished chieftain, Gen. Santa Anna, to the numberless encroachments and infractions which have been made by the present administration upon the constitution and laws of our adopted and beloved country.

Resolved, That as *freemen* devoted to a correct interpretation, and enforcement of the constitution and laws, according to their true spirit. We pledge our lives and fortunes in support of the same, and of the distinguished leader, who is now so gallantly fighting in defence of civil liberty.

Resolved, That the people of Texas be invited to co-operate with us in support of the principles incorporated in the foregoing resolutions.

The citizens of Brazoria and of the precinct of Victoria in this colony also pronounced in favour of said plan. A deputation was sent to Lieut. Col. Ugartecha the commandant of Velasco, inviting him to adhere to said plan, which he refused. This left those who had pronounced no alternative but to attack him; they did so on the 27th June, under the command of the 2d Alcalde of this jurisdiction, John Austin, and after a bloody battle in which the most determined bravery was displayed on both sides, the fort surrendered to the *Santa Anna forces,* and not to a faction of rebels against the nation, as had been erroneously stated by the enemies of Texas and of its inhabitants.

It is due to Lieut. Col. Ugartecha and but justice to say, that the only complaint against him was that he sent a re-inforcement of troops and arms to Col. Bradburn and that he refused to adhere to the plan of Vera Cruz. He acted under the orders of Col. Bradburn, and was bound by his duty as a subordinate officer, to obey him, and do as he did. No one has attached blame or censure to him, and the same men who attacked fort Velasco, embraced him most cordially the moment the conflict ended as a personal friend, whom they esteemed and respected for his moral worth and bravery. Every attention and respect which circumstances would permit was shown to him, his officers and troops: it was, in fact, a political conflict between citizens acknowledging the same national flag.

The Ayuntamiento of the jurisdiction of Austin, were impressed with the importance of preserving the public tranquillity, and felt the peculiarly delicate situation of the settlers of these colonies, owing to their being of foreign birth. It was well known that every species of calumny had been heaped upon them by the enemies of Texas, and of a republican and enlightened emigration, with the design of reviving amongst the Mexicans the old Spanish prejudices, against persons born in another country. It was feared that those enemies would take advantage of any disturbances here, to pervert the truth and attribute to them hostile views against the Mexican territory and federal constitution. This body was under the immediate eye and direction of the political chief of the department, who was then in this town and equally anxious to preserve the public tranquillity; and who we are assured is as much opposed to military encroachments as any other man in the community. It will also be remembered that the Ayuntamiento had no means of acquiring information as to the true state of things in the interior of this republic, the only newspaper that was permitted to reach here through the post office department, was the ministerial "Registro Official"—under these circumstances, this body used every effort to preserve good order and keep the settlers from participating in the present civil war, and it is probable that these efforts would have been successful, had not events been precipitated in the manner they have been by the tyrannical and illegal acts of Col. Bradburn. But now as public opinion has expressed itself in the most decided and unequivocal manner, in favour of the plan of Vera Cruz, the same reasons which prevented the Ayuntamiento from taking an early lead in this question, have impelled that body, to unite with the people in adhering to said plan; which reasons are the preservation of harmony and the advancement of the general good which can alone be effected by the most perfect union. In consideration of all which and being convinced that the objects of the political party, who, on the 2d of January last, proclaimed the plan of Vera Cruz, are to restore the government to the true constitutional basis, and to make it in practice what it professes to be in theory—a free republican constitutional confederation of sovereign states; the Ayuntamiento and citizens of the jurisdiction of Austin, have adopted the following resolutions:

First—That they solemnly adhere to the said plan of Vera Cruz and to the principles of the republican party headed by Gen. Antonio Lopez de Santa Anna.

Second—That the inhabitants of this colony have never for one moment deviated from their duty as Mexican citizens, that in adopting the plan of Vera Cruz, they have no other object in view, than to contribute their feeble voice and aid in sustaining the constitution and the true dignity and decorum of the national flag, and the rights of the state of Coahuila and Texas, which have been insulted by military encroachments in these colonies since 1830, and that they will be at all times ready to take up arms in defence of the independence and constitution of their adopted country and the integrity of its territory.

Third—That the general and state constitutions ought to be rigorously observed as the only guarantee for public tranquillity and national freedom, and past abuses corrected.

Fourth—That the liberty of the press ought to be established without any censorship or restriction whatever, other than a recourse of the judicial tribunal in case of personal slander.

Fifth—That all citizens ought to be subjected to the same laws and the same tribunals for civil offences; thus destroying all privileged orders which are repugnant to a republic.

Sixth—That conciliatory measures ought to be adopted to put an end to the present civil war on a basis that will effectually guarantee the security and rights of all persons who have taken part on either side and prevent the recurrence of similar difficulties by adapting the laws and the administration of the government to the genuine principles of the federal republican system.

Seventh—That a large standing army is totally unnecessary for national defence, in the present state of friendly relations between Mexico and all foreign powers except Spain, which latter, it is well known is too impotent to attack her; that such an army is a burthen to the people and consumes the revenue of the nation without any benefit; that it endangers the national liberty and is continually disturbing the public tranquillity by affording the means of committing and defending despotic acts and producing revolutions.

Eighth—That the measures of the administration since 1830, have been directed to embarrass and retard emigration from foreign countries, rather than promote and encourage it; thus paralyzing the advancement of the nation, and preventing the settlement of its uninhabited and wild lands, to the evident injury of the national prosperity.

Ninth—That a copy of this act shall be delivered to Col. Jose Antonio Mexia, an officer of the liberating army, now in Texas, with a request that he will transmit the same to his excellency, the commander-in-chief, Gen. Santa Anna, with the assurances of the respect and hearty co-operation of the inhabitants of this colony, in the glorious work of political regeneration, in which he is engaged.

Tenth—That a copy of this act shall be transmitted to each Ayuntamiento in Texas, and to the chief of the department of Bexar, to be forwarded to the Governor of the state, in order that his excellency may be pleased to use his influence with the legislature, whom we respectfully petition to take under consideration the principles expressed in said act, and to adopt such measures as in their judgment will tend to restore the tranquillity of the confederacy, and protect the rights of the state.

The foregoing exposition and resolutions were unanimously adopted by the Ayuntamiento and citizens convened in general meeting, in the town of San Felipe de Austin, 27th July, 1832.

Documents and publications, explanatory of the late commotions and present state of affairs in Austin's Colony.

On the 16th inst. Col. Jose Antonio Mexia, the 2d officer of the 2d division of the liberating army of Gen. Santa Anna under the command of Gen. Montezuma, anchored off the mouth of the Brazos river with his fleet and forces composed of five sail and four hundred men. Col. Mexia sailed from Tampico on the 22d ultimo to attack the ministerial forces at Matamoras, and which place he took on the 29th as will be seen by the translation from the Boletin inserted below. Being informed at Matamoras by the intercepted correspondence from fort Velasco, and other places in Texas, of the movements here, which were attributed by the military commandants of those posts to have for their objects the separation of Texas from Mexico, he agreed to a cessation of arms with Col. Guera, on the 6th of this month, and on the 14th sailed from the Brazos Santiago for Texas, accompanied by Col. S. F. Austin, our representative in the state legislature and founder of this colony. Immediately on his arrival, Col. Mexia, addressed an official letter to the Alcalde, John Austin, which is published below with the answer, and in conjunction with the other documents, will give the public an account of what has transpired.

Sir—I have the honour to enclose you a copy of the convention entered into, between the commandants in chief of Matamoras and myself on the 6th of the present month.* This document will inform you of the motives which brought me to Texas, and what would have been my course, had the late movements here been directed against the integrity of the national territory.

But if, as I have been assured by respectable citizens, the past occurrences were on account of the colonists having adhered to the plan of Vera Cruz, and I am officially informed of that fact in an unequivocal manner, you can in that case apprise the inhabitants that I will unite with them to accomplish their wishes, and that the forces under my command will protect their adhesion to said plan. This occasion affords me the opportunity of presenting to you the assurance of my consideration and respect.

God and Liberty, off the mouth of the Brazos river on board the brig of war Gen. Santa Anna.

JOSE ANTONIO MEXIA.

To citizen John Austin, Alcalde, 16th July, 1832.

Answer of the Alcalde, John Austin, to the foregoing.

Sir—I have received your official letter dated 10th of the present month, and in reply, have the honour to inform

---

* This convention was made between Col. Jose Mariano Guerra, commandant-in-chief of Matamoras, and Col. Mexia, on the 6th July for a cessation of arms, and Col. Mexia agreed to proceed with his fleet and forces to Texas, to protect the Mexican territory which it was stated by the official reports made from fort Velasco and other places, was endangered by the attempt of the colonists to declare the country independent.

you, that a committee appointed by the inhabitants of this
town, will present you copies of the acts and resolutions
heretofore adopted, and the documents to the past occurrences, which will explain to you the principles that have
governed us up to this time. These documents contain our
true sentiments, and will serve as an answer to your official
letter to me, dated the 16th of this month.

The enemies of Texas, the enemies of the enterprising
men who have devoted their time and labours to improve a
country that was never before trod by civilized men, have
taken pains and are continually doing it, to attribute to us
a disposition to separate from the Mexican confederation.
We have not entertained and have not any such intention or
desire. We are Mexicans by adoption, we are the same in
hearts and will so remain. If the laws have granted to us
the honourable title of citizens, we wish that title should
be respected, and that the authorities established by the
constitution of the state, shall govern us. We are farmers
and not soldiers, and therefore desire, that the military
commandants shall not interfere with us at all. Since 1830,
we have been pretty much governed militarily, and in so
despotic a manner, that we were finally driven to arms, to
restrain within their limits, the military subalterns of the
general government. We have not insulted the flag of our
adopted country, as has been falsely stated by our enemies,
but on the contrary, we have defended and sustained its
true dignity, and attacked those who have outraged it, by
using it as a pretext for their encroachments upon the constitution and sovereignty of the state of Coahuila and Texas,
and as a cover for their baseness and personal crimes. The
commandant of fort Velasco, acted under the orders of the
commandant of Anahuac, Col. Juan Davis Bradburn who
was his superior. An investigation of the conduct of this
officer at Anahuac, will inform you fully of the details of
many despotic and arbitrary acts. He refused to respect
the authorities or the constitution of the state of Coahuila
and Texas, or to adhere to the plan of Vera Cruz which
we had adopted. He was sustained by the commandant of
the Nacogdoches, Col. Predras, and by that of fort Velasco,
Lieut. Col. Ugartecha, and consequently we were compelled
to oppose them all. Col. Ugartecha was invited by a committee appointed for that purpose to espouse the plan of
Vera Cruz. He refused to do so, and we attacked fort
Velasco, on the 27th of last month, with 120 farmers hastily

collected, without discipline and badly armed. And after an obstinate and bloody engagement of 11 hours, it capitulated on the terms expressed in the enclosed copy of the capitulation, every article of which has been strictly complied with on our part, besides furnishing him with the provisions he needed for his troops. I herewith furnish you a return of the killed and wounded.

This, sir, is what passed. I hope it will be sufficient to convince you, that these inhabitants have not manifested any other desire or intention, than to unite with Gen. Santa Anna, to procure the establishment of peace in the republic, under the shield of the constitution and laws—and that the sovereignty of the states shall be respected.

It is a matter of pride and congratulation to me, that you have come to this place, to see, with your own eyes, the rectitude of our sentiments, and that it has afforded us the opportunity of presenting to you our respects; and the assurances of our hearty co-operation in the great and glorious cause which is so nobly advocated by our distinguished commander-in-chief, Gen. Santa Anna. God and Liberty.

JOHN AUSTIN.

To citizen Col. JOSE ANTONIO MEXIA. ⎱
Brazoria, July 18, 1832. ⎰

Col. Antonio Mexia—SIR—Conformable to your request that a report should be made you of the number of men killed and wounded, in the attack upon fort Velasco—and the wounded left with us by the commandant at that post, Col. Ugartecha, together with an account of the provisions furnished him, and a return of the arms and munitions taken with the fort.

We hand you separate reports and returns of the same.

We have it not in our power to give you any light upon the request, that "a report of those killed in the fort should be annexed," but refer you to the minutes of Col. Ugartecha on that subject.

With consideration, &c.

JOHN AUSTIN, Commandant.

Return of arms and ammunition taken at fort Velasco, 26th June, 1832.

35 stand of arms in bad order, wanting locks, bayonets, &c.; 1 brass cannon, eight pounder; 1 small iron swivel;

14

30 cartridges for the cannon; 45 do. for the swivel; 200 do. for muskets; 40 cartouch boxes; 2 brass blunderbusses.

Return of the wounded from fort Velasco, left in our care by the commandant Lieut. Col. Ugartecha.

2 sergeants, under medical treatment; 5 privates; 1 since dead.

Return of the killed and wounded on the part of the citizens pronounced in favour of the plans of Gen. Santa Anna, in the attack upon fort Velasco.

7 men killed; 6 badly wounded, under medical aid; 11 slightly wounded.

Translation.

An agreement, which by order of Lieut. Col. Domingo Ugartecha, we the two officers, commissioned by said chief, form with the division of the colonists who declare in favour of the plan formed by the garrison of Vera Cruz, which duplicate, Messrs. W. J. Russel, and W. H. Wharton, signed on the part of the colonists, under the following articles:

First—The garrison will be permitted to march out with all the honours of war, that is to say, with their arms, ammunition and baggage.

Second—There shall be a vessel made ready for their embarkation to Matamoras, they paying to the captain of the same, 600 dollars for the voyage.

Third—If the collector, Don Francisco Duclor, should wish to embark, he may do so, the Sargt. Ignatus Lopez, and two soldiers, who remain with the former, shall be suffered to come and incorporate themselves.

Fourth—All the wounded military of the garrison who can march, shall carry arms, and those who cannot, must remain to be cured, receive good treatment and hospitality, being supplied with food, which will be satisfied by the nation.

Fifth—The 600 dollars, which the captain of the vessel is to receive, shall be free of duties, and the troops shall be disembarked outside the bar of the Brazos Santiago.

Sixth—Lieut. Col. citizen Domingo Ugartecha, the two officers who sign, and the ensign Don Emanuel Pintardo, remain by this treaty, obliged not to return to take arms, against the expressed plan above cited—formed under the orders of Gen. Antonia Lopez de Santa Anna, and by the garrison of Vera Cruz.

Seventh—This day at 11 o'clock in the morning, will be ready, the schooner, Brazoria, in which the garrison of the fort is to embark, but previous to her going to sea, the schooner Elizabeth, should arrive at this point, the garrison shall be put on board the latter.

Eighth—The cannon of eight, and the swivel gun, shall remain at fort Velasco, with all the public stores, supernumerary guns and ammunition.

Ninth—All sorts of provisions, after the garrison shall have taken what may be necessary for its march, are to remain in the fort, at the disposal of the owners, given the corresponding promissory notes, that their pay may be satisfactorily made to the captain of the transporting vessel, who shall carry the power of the owners for the recovery of their import.

Camp at the mouth of the river Brazos, June 29th, 1832.

JUAN MORET,
JOSE MARIA RINCON,
W. H. WHARTON,
W. J. RUSSELL.

I approve of the above agreement of peace, and will observe it.   DOMINGODE UGARTECHA.

I approve of the above agreement of peace, and will observe it.   JOHN AUSTIN.

Proceedings of a public meeting.

At a large and respectable meeting of the citizens of the precinct of Victoria, convened according to public notice, on the 16th of July—they unanimously resolved to succeed or perish in the cause of the constitution and SANTA ANNA, or in other words, the plan of Vera Cruz.

The meeting then proceeded to elect a committee of vigilance for the promotion of their cause—when the following gentlemen were elected:

W. D. C. HALL,
HENRY SMITH,
W. H. WHARTON,
J. P. CALDWELL,
P. D. McNEEL.

Who subsequently elected Charles B. Stewart their Secretary.

On the night of the same day the committee learning the arrival of Col. Mexia, a friend and officer of Gen. Santa Anna, at our port from Matamoras with a fleet of five vessels, accompanied by Col. Austin, bringing us the joyful intelligence of the success of our cause, and of the surrender of Matamoras.

Appointed a deputation to wait on, and invite him to Brazoria. He acceded and arrived in town on Tuesday evening, July 17th, in company with Col. Austin.

On their arrival on the east bank of the Brazos, they were saluted with the firing of three cannon, and after partaking of some refreshments at Maj. Brighams, crossed the river, at the bank of which, they were received by the committee and by two of the signers of the Turtle Bayou resolutions, who were present, Capt. Wiley Martin and Luke Lessasier, and conducted to an arch erected for the purpose, and saluted by one gun, when W. H. Wharton, read the following address:

Colonel Mexia—As a member of a committee appointed by the inhabitants of the precinct of Victoria to congratulate your arrival, I tender you in the name of those I represent, a cordial and heart-felt welcome among us, we view you as a fellow struggler in the same field with ourselves, and as the harbinger of the happy intelligence, that the cause of the constitution and Santa Anna, or in other words, the cause of truth and justice, and liberty, has triumphed most signally and gloriously, we hail the day of your arrival amongst us, in the sacred cause you came to advocate, as the brightest one that ever shone on the prospects of Texas. We long groaned and languished under the withering influence of the *odious and obnoxious law of the sixth of April*, a murmur, not that we did not perceive its ruinous effects upon us, but that situated as we were, we feared it might seem indelicate and dictatorial in us to take the lead in opposition to the arbitrary measures of the late tramplers on the constitution, when, however, the highly distinguished Gen. Santa Anna, arose as the hero and vindicator of liberty and the constitution; we may feel as if a brighter and happier era had dawned upon our prospects, and as if we were then justified, and indeed in duty to ourselves, called upon to go heart and hand with him, in his righteous cause. We did go with him, and not twenty-four hours elapsed, since in numerous and public meetings, we resolved to succeed or perish with him. We declared for his cause, sir, when it was in doubt, and that it is triumphant, we give you the most solemn of pledges, that in putting down the present violators of the constitution, and bringing the government back to a strictly legitimate mode of procedure, Gen. Santa Anna, shall have our warmest support, and our most zealous co-operation. In conclusion, sir, I tender you a warm, sincere and unanimous welcome. And to you, Col. Austin, I am likewise instructed to offer our cordial congratulation on your safe return amongst us. In the arduous scenes in which we have lately acted, we all wished for your counsel and co-operation, we were deprived of this, but we still are gratified, that we are once more together at so propitious a period as the present.

To which Col. Mexia, made the following reply.

GENTLEMEN—It is most gratifying to me to see your devotion to the Mexican confederation, to the constitution, and to his excellency, Gen. LOPEZ DE SANTA ANNA. Men who are governed by their principles, cannot be called enemies of mine, for being myself influenced by the same, I should do an injustice, did I not believe, that I was amongst friends and brothers, whom I ought to appreciate. We are all actuated by the same common sympathies, springing from the uniformity of our sentiments.

The principles defended by you, are the same which we have proclaimed in Vera Cruz and Tampico. Federation laws, and a liberal ministry, who will respect the general constitution and the sovereignty of the states. This is the basis of the plan of Gen. SANTA ANNA, and that in future, the law and not individual caprice shall govern. SANTA ANNA asks nothing for himself, but all for his country.

He has always sustained the cause of the people, and the nation will see him return to private life, the moment government is legalized, and the constitution restored to its full vigour, so that the citizens may enjoy the blessings of the system they have adopted.

When Col. Austin rose and remarked.

I return my sincere thanks for your kind and cordial welcome. Nothing could have been more gratifying to me, than to have participated with you in the arduous scenes in

14*

which you have lately acted, and to have contributed my feeble aid, in the cause you have so nobly and *bravely* advocated.

During my absence, I have never for one moment lost sight of the interests of my constituents in Texas, and have used every effort to advocate and protect them, which circumstances and the situations I have been placed in, would permit. I will continue to do the same, and my fellow citizens of this colony, can command my feeble services now, and at all times when they deem them necessary.

After which a further salute of 21 guns, a *feu-de-joi*, from one of the companies, who were in the action at fort Velasco, were fired, when the colonels were escorted to the residence of *John Austin, Esq. second Alcalde,* by a numerous body of our citizens, who on returning to town, manifested their joyful feelings by *illuminations, bon-fires, firing of cannon, &c.,* all the night.

Meeting of July 18th, attended by Col. Mexia.

Col. Mexia, having expressed a desire to have our motives and actions explained to him, that he might make due representations to his chief. The citizens convened for that purpose on the next evening, (July 18th,) at three o'clock, when Luke Lessasier and W. D. C. Hall, read him the following expositions of our acts, motives and feelings, and delivered him these documents, as the sum and matter of our operations from the date of our taking up arms against the post of *Anahuac,* to the present time.

Col. JOSE ANTONIO MEXIA—SIR—Having understood that the cause which impelled us to take up arms, have been misrepresented, or misunderstood, we therefore make you the following representation:

The colonists of Texas, have long since been convinced of the arbitrary and unconstitutional measures of the administration of Bustamente, as evinced.

First—By their repeated violations of the constitution and laws, and their total disregard of the civil and political rights of the people.

Second—By their fixing and establishing among us, in time of peace, military posts, the officers of which totally disregarding the local civil authorities of the state; and by committing various acts, which evinced opposition to the true interests of the people in the enjoyment of civil liberty.

Third—By the arrest of Juan Francisco Madero, the commissioner on the part of the state government, to put the inhabitants east of the river Trinity, in possession of their lands in conformity with the laws of colonization.

Fourth—By the interposition of a military force, preventing the Alcalde of the jurisdiction of liberty, from the exercise of his constitutional functions.

Fifth—By appointing to the revenue department of Galveston, a man whose character for infamy had been clearly established, and made known to the government, and whose principles were avowedly inimical to the true interests of the people of Texas.

Sixth—By the military commandant of Anahuac advising and procuring servants to quit the service of their masters, offering them protection, causing them to labour for his individual benefit by force, and refusing to compensate master or servant.

Seventh—By the imprisonment of our citizens without lawful cause, and claiming the right of trying said citizens by a military court, for offences of a character alone cognizable by the civil authority; and by refusing to deliver them over to the said authority when demanded.

Such Col. Mexia, are the causes which impelled us to take up arms, and the following declarations are the legitimate offspring of our deliberations, and form the basis of all our acts.

This declaration is embodied in the expositions made by the Ayuntamiento, on the 27th July.

Col. JOSE ANTONIO MEXIA—SIR—As chairman of a committee, elected by the inhabitants of the precinct of Victoria, I respectfully represent to you, that some time in the early part of June, the people of this precinct received information that the colonists assembled before Anahuac had declared for the constitution and Gen. Santa Anna. We were rejoiced to see this declaration, for such had been for a long time, our own feelings and wishes.

For a long time we had groaned under the arbitrary acts of Bustamente's administration. We had been convinced that that administration was disregardful of the constitution, that it was hostile to the most vital interests of the colonists, as was sufficiently evinced among other things, by their odious law of the 6th of April, and by the establishing of numerous garrisons amongst us in time of peace; which garrisons always trampled upon the civil authority, and upon the constitutional rights and privileges of our citizens. The people of this precinct, therefore, immediately met and concurred in the declaration for the constitution, and Santa Anna. When this was done, we felt ourselves in open opposition to all the officers, civil and military of the government, against which he had declared.

To declare against a government and to permit its officers to remain unmolested at our very doors, would be inconsistent and ridiculous; we therefore proceeded to displace the collector of the customs at Brazoria, and to reduce the nearest garrison, which was that at the mouth of the Brazos.

In all that we have done, we have cried out and fought for the constitution and Gen. Santa Anna, its defender. We have conceived, and do conceive the constitution to be a liberal, enlightened and republican instrument, and have, therefore, never raised a voice or an arm against it.

We have understood, however, that it has gone abroad, that we have been declaring and battling for independence. This is slanderous of us, and we wish you as our friend, so to represent it to Gen. Santa Anna, and at the same time, to assure him, that an administration guided by the constitution, will find as warm and as loyal support among the colonists of Texas, as any other part of the Mexican republic. W. D. C. HALL.

At the conclusion of which address, Mr. Wharton made the following remark:

Col. MEXIA, in order to show you, tha twe had not declared independence, as had been misrepresented to you; that we were not battling for ourselves; we refer you to the manner in which we were recognized by the commandant of fort Velasco, in the treaty between him and ourselves, on his capitulation. By a perusal of which treaty, it will be clearly seen that he recognized us as the favourers and supporters of the plan of Vera Cruz. Whilst on the subject of Col. Ugartecha, we beg leave to say, that in his official and private intercourse with us prior to the battle, he satisfied us all, that he was a friend and a gentleman, and that during the conflict which ended in the capitulation, he acted most heroically.

This much we consider due to real merit and praiseworthy valour.

Col. MEXIA, then rose and addressed the meeting as follows:

Gentlemen—The official note which I addressed to the Alcalde, under date of the 16th inst. and the printed document which accompanied it, has informed you of my sentiments, and what were the motives which caused my visit to Texas.

The late occurrences produced by the causes which the committee and the president have just explained, were represented in a very different light from the true one. It was stated and repeated by the official reports made by the commandants of three military posts to their supreme chief, that the object of the inhabitants of these colonies, was to separate from the Mexican confederation, and declare themselves independent. As a Mexican, I could not look on with indifference when the territories of my nation was attacked, and forming an armistice with my adversary, I offered to aid the authorities of this province against those who had attacked it with such intentions. The printed document before mentioned by me, explains this part of the subject.

I sailed from Matamoras with the fleet and forces under my command, and in 40 hours anchored off the bar of this river where I informed myself of the nature of the late occurrences.

These inhabitants have had their meetings with that republican frankness, which characterises them, they have adopted the resolutions, which you have presented to me, adhering to the plan of Vera Cruz, sustained by Gen. Santa Anna as the chief. The cause which you have thus adopted is that of the people against oppression; that of the friends of federal institutions, against the military and oppressive government which the ministers of Gen. Bustamente wished to establish. These being the principles which influence this respectable community, I should be inconsistent with my own, were I not to offer them my friendship, and the support of the chiefs under whose orders I am acting.

Until affairs are settled in the interior which has been in commotion from the same causes that have produced the confusion here. I recommend peace, harmony and union, to effect which you will find me disposed to contribute my support.

Translation from the Boletin at Matamoras.

On the 26th of the present month, at 4 o'clock in the afternoon, Col. Jose Antonio Mexia, disembarked at the

Brazos Santiago with his forces; Lieut. Col. Alexander Yhari, with a force of forty men, prepared to oppose him, but the brave chief of the detachment, of the liberating army, advanced in a pilot boat, took the schooner Juanita, anchored within pistol shot of the point occupied by Yhari, and covered the landing of his troops from the launches. As soon as the landing was effected, Yhari was invited to pronounce for SANTA ANNA, which he refused to do, but his troops immediately proclaimed the plan of the free, and with enthusiasm joined their standard.

Immediately after taking possession of the Brazos Santiago, a party of one hundred infantry with two pieces of artillery, marched to Bocachiea, where they raised an entrenchment; on the 27th, the force was augmented by a number of the military and citizens who hastened with delight to sustain the cause of the *free*, or perish in the attempt.

On the 28th, a party of 54 or 60 cavalry was discovered approaching, and it was the desire of the commander-in-chief not to engage them, although he knew the obstinacy of the officer, Don Ignacio Rodriguez, who commanded them, and who retired with his troops and occupied a position on the main road.

On the 29th, after leaving a competent force to protect the brig of war, Santa Anna, and the armed schooner Montazuma of Vera Cruz, Montazuma of Tampico, Adela and Ameria; and also guards to the fortifications at the Brazos Santiago, and Boca Chica, the troops marched for this town. Lieut. Rodriguez wished to dispute the passage, notwithstanding the invitations he received from Col. Mexia to avoid the effusion of blood, and it became necessary to open a passage by force. Measures were adopted to do so, and at the third discharge of the cannon Rodriguez's men abandoned him, and joined the lines of Col. Mexia, with Lieut. Gonzalos at their head, having refused to fight against the holy cause of liberty, and previously wished Rodriguez to join the same cause—at the same time, a party of 40 infantry of the 11th battalion, joined Col. Mexia's division. Col. Guerra with the troops in this town, Lojero and others, well known for their anti-liberal principles, precipitately fled, giving the most barbarous orders to his troops, such as to bayonet the pack-mules loaded with the baggage and ammunition, should they be overtaken.

Col. Mexia's division of the liberating army, is therefore in full possession of this town, increased by a great number who have joined it. The utmost tranquillity prevails, the inhabitants are tranquil, because they now see the falsehood of what had been stated by the enemies of the cause which was proclaimed by the heroic conqueror of Tampico, Gen. ANTONIO LOPES DE SANTA ANNA.

The Far Western Frontier

An Arno Press Collection

[Angel, Myron, editor]. **History of Nevada.** 1881.

Barnes, Demas. **From the Atlantic to the Pacific, Overland.** 1866.

Beadle, J[ohn] H[anson]. **The Undeveloped West; Or, Five Years in the Territories.** [1873].

Bidwell, John. **Echoes of the Past:** An Account of the First Emigrant Train to California. [1914].

Bowles, Samuel. **Our New West.** 1869.

Browne, J[ohn] Ross. **Adventures in the Apache Country.** 1871.

Browne, J[ohn] Ross. **Report of the Debates in the Convention of California, on the Formation of the State Constitution.** 1850.

Byers, W[illiam] N. and J[ohn] H. Kellom. **Hand Book to the Gold Fields of Nebraska and Kansas.** 1859.

Carvalho, S[olomon] N. **Incidents of Travel and Adventure in the Far West; with Col. Fremont's Last Expedition Across the Rocky Mountains.** 1857.

Clayton, William. **William Clayton's Journal.** 1921.

Cooke, P[hilip] St. G[eorge]. **Scenes and Adventures in the Army.** 1857.

Cornwallis, Kinahan. **The New El Dorado; Or, British Columbia.** 1858.

Davis, W[illiam] W. H. **El Gringo; Or, New Mexico and Her People.** 1857.

De Quille, Dan. (William Wright). **A History of the Comstock Silver Lode & Mines.** 1889.

Delano, A[lonzo]. **Life on the Plains and Among the Diggings;** Being Scenes and Adventures of an Overland Journey to California. 1854.

Ferguson, Charles D. **The Experiences of a Forty-niner in California.** (Originally published as *The Experiences of a Forty-niner During Thirty-four Years' Residence in California and Australia*). 1888.

Forbes, Alexander. **California:** A History of Upper and Lower California. 1839.

Fossett, Frank. **Colorado:** Its Gold and Silver Mines, Farms and Stock Ranges, and Health and Pleasure Resorts. 1879.

The Gold Mines of California: Two Guidebooks. 1973.

Gray, W[illiam] H[enry]. **A History of Oregon, 1792–1849.** 1870.

Green, Thomas J. **Journal of the Texian Expedition Against Mier.** 1845.

Henry, W[illiam] S[eaton]. **Campaign Sketches of the War with Mexico.** 1847.

[Hildreth, James]. **Dragoon Campaigns to the Rocky Mountains.** 1836.

Hines, Gustavus. **Oregon:** Its History, Condition and Prospects. 1851.

Holley, Mary Austin. **Texas:** Observations, Historical, Geographical and Descriptive. 1833.

Hollister, Ovando J[ames]. **The Mines of Colorado.** 1867.

Hughes, John T. **Doniphan's Expedition.** 1847.

Johnston, W[illiam] G. **Experiences of a Forty-niner.** 1892.

Jones, Anson. **Memoranda and Official Correspondence Relating to the Republic of Texas, Its History and Annexation.** 1859.

Kelly, William. **An Excursion to California Over the Prairie, Rocky Mountains, and Great Sierra Nevada.** 1851. 2 Volumes in 1.

Lee, D[aniel] and J[oseph] H. Frost. **Ten Years in Oregon.** 1844.

Macfie, Matthew. **Vancouver Island and British Columbia.** 1865.

Marsh, James B. **Four Years in the Rockies; Or, the Adventures of Isaac P. Rose.** 1884.

Mowry, Sylvester. **Arizona and Sonora:** The Geography, History, and Resources of the Silver Region of North America. 1864.

Mullan, John. **Miners and Travelers' Guide to Oregon, Washington, Idaho, Montana, Wyoming, and Colorado.** 1865.

Newell, C[hester]. **History of the Revolution in Texas.** 1838.

Parker, A[mos] A[ndrew]. **Trip to the West and Texas.** 1835.

Pattie, James O[hio]. **The Personal Narrative of James O. Pattie, of Kentucky.** 1831.

Rae, W[illiam] F[raser]. **Westward by Rail:** The New Route to the East. 1871.

Ryan, William Redmond. **Personal Adventures in Upper and Lower California, in 1848–9.** 1850/1851. 2 Volumes in 1.

Shaw, William. **Golden Dreams and Waking Realities:** Being the Adventures of a Gold-Seeker in California and the Pacific Islands. 1851.

Stuart, Granville. **Montana As It Is:** Being a General Description of its Resources. 1865.

Texas in 1840, Or the Emigrant's Guide to the New Republic. 1840.

Thornton, J. Quinn. **Oregon and California in 1848.** 1849. 2 Volumes in 1.

Upham, Samuel C. **Notes of a Voyage to California via Cape Horn, Together with Scenes in El Dorado, in the Years 1849–'50.** 1878.

Woods, Daniel B. **Sixteen Months at the Gold Diggings.** 1851.

Young, F[rank] G., editor. **The Correspondence and Journals of Captain Nathaniel J. Wyeth, 1831–6.** 1899.